UNIQUELY CRETE

Life Redefined On A Greek Island

by

MELANIE A. CRANE

UNIQUELY CRETE

Copyright © 2019 by Melanie Crane

Illumify Media Global
www.IllumifyMedia.com
"Write. Market. Publish. *SELL!*"

Paperback ISBN: 978-1-949021-17-2
eBook ISBN: 978-1-949021-18-9

Printed in the United States of America
16 17 18 19 20 21 LSI 9 8 7 6 5 4 3 2 1

AUTHOR'S BIO

Melanie first started writing when her life took a turn and she found herself living on an island in the middle of the Mediterranean Sea. Her tales of off-the-beaten-track places and heartwarming stories of the people that populate them were originally recorded in her photo travel blog, *Cretan Chronicles*.

Before she was a writer she was a musician, teacher, and typical parent of two lively kids that kept her close to home. Now an empty nester, she has developed an insatiable appetite for travel and the perfect cup of espresso (preferably enjoyed together with her husband.) She enjoys advising other wanderers about the merits of "slow travel" and her current blog, *Wander, Linger, Savor* can be viewed on her website. When she's not traveling, she can be found at home, relishing in everything the Colorado Rocky Mountains have to offer.

You can visit her website to view photos of the places she references in this book and learn more about her travels beyond Crete.

melanieacrane.com

ACKNOWLEDGEMENTS

Many thanks to . . .

My Dad, for teaching me that traveling with vision means giving back more than you take.

And my Mom, for always being a safe harbor to come home to.

Brandon and Holly, for giving me wings after I gave them theirs. My most treasured journey was the years spent being your mom.

All my precious brothers and sisters in Christ at the Hania Apostolic Church, especially Mike and Tippy who mentored us with wisdom, compassion and tender love.

Marina and Nick, for all the smiles, laughs, tears and prayers that have made our friendship one that transcends time and distance.

Cameron and Shelby, our Farkel, Frappe, foodie friends for the mostly spontaneous hours of fun and games every week, and for being our closest friends and partners in crime during the years we spent together on a crazy island.

The whole Kabutz clan: What a privilege to be included in your fold, to be invited into your home, to be a part of the childrens' lives as they grew up . . . Maxi, Connie and Bangie, Efi, it's your fault that I was always smiling. Heinz, you took the idea of a BBQ to a whole new level the same as Helene took my walk with God.

Our expat community of friends from a myriad of diverse cultures who made our Crete experience both bearable and beautiful.

Courtney Drysdale for her boundless creativity in creating my website and the patience in helping me navigate the unknown territories of social media marketing.

DEDICATION

For Richard – my Northern Star

CONTENTS

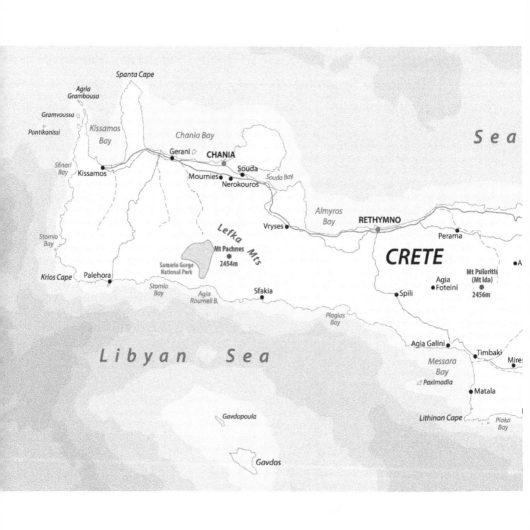

To everything there is a season,
a time for every purpose under heaven."

Ecclesiastes 3:1

PREFACE

I looked out the window of the airplane and strained to focus on the green and blue beneath me. My view of the island that had been my temporary home became obscured by clouds, or was it tears? This island reminded me of silk on stone, not just in its landscape defined by soft, luxurious water and hard, rugged earth, but in something deeper—a soul soothed and beaten and soothed again like waves battering and then caressing the rocky shores of Crete.

The events of the last month had left me exhausted, emotionally and physically. Part of me desperately wanted to escape, back to my island where daily life was at best, heavenly, and at worst, aggravating. But waiting on the other side of the ocean was a family in crisis; broken, bleeding and devastated. And so, we were headed home to Colorado, and I couldn't get there soon enough.

I didn't know what the future held, but I was sure that the past had prepared me for it. Lessons learned in Crete would sustain me. Living on this island, with all its beauty and chaos, had shaped me into a different person. When we moved to Crete, I was sure God had some big changes in mind for us, but I could have never imagined how deep those changes would go. Years later, my faith in God, myself, and in others was completely redefined like the dry landscape after a soaking life-giving rain. And now, I faced another storm of life, another test of faith; But I was prepared. After all, I had seen beauty rising out of the impossible and renewed life from tiny seeds of faith.

I had witnessed the harmony of life and death on an island in the sea.

INTRODUCTION

"To move, to breathe, to fly, to float,
To gain all while you give,
To roam the roads of lands remote,
To travel is to live."

—Hans Christian Andersen

"Do you want to move to Crete?"

I heard my husband's words, but their meaning didn't register with me. I had just started to boil the pasta for dinner when he walked in the door from a long day at work. Anticipating the typical afterwork conversation around the day's events, I'd expected to hear a different question. Like "How was your day?" or "What's for dinner?" Instead, Richard dropped a bomb.

I froze. Forgetting the pasta on the stove, I tried to think, *Where in the world is Crete?* We had talked about living overseas, perhaps Germany or Italy, but Crete? With the pasta boiling on the stove, I ran for the atlas. Crete was a Mediterranean island I hadn't heard about since sixth-grade geography class. There it was, floating on the blue page, suspended between Greece and the continent of Africa. My eyes measured the distance between Colorado and Crete. *So FAR*, I thought. *So DIFFERENT.*

I have a love affair with maps: Old out-of-date ones or slick, still-crispy new ones. It doesn't matter what condition they're in, as long as there's a longitude and latitude, I'm mesmerized. Wanderlust is in my family genes. My father was constantly on the move, traveling for business and making it pleasure. The more exotic the destination, the better. He came home with stories of magical places and the people who populated them. His memories were the wings under my imagination from a young age. But moving to a Mediterranean island was never on my radar, and definitely beyond my imagination.

We barely noticed the overcooked pasta as we nibbled at our dinner that evening in April 2009. Instead, we devoured any information we could find about Crete. Richard explained his job offer with the US Navy as I searched the computer for photos and maps of the island. Over the next few days and weeks, both of us obsessed over Crete. We went back and forth, wavering like two small ships on the great sea that surrounded the island. We deliberated hard and prayed harder, measuring the pros and cons. In the end, we gave in to the consistent nagging feeling that was growing inside both of us: We need to do this. What would we miss if we didn't go?

The adventure began as soon as we made the decision. In July of 2009, we forged ahead with all the details of an overseas move. My ever-growing to-do list included de-cluttering, organizing, and prioritizing our household goods. The real challenge was juggling more important items like patience, focus, and sanity. It was a seesaw of ups and downs that not only taxed our brains but stretched our emotions as well.

We broke the news to our families and friends little by little. Their reactions were as different as their personalities. Most were excited for us, and others were incredulous that we would even consider leaving Colorado. When we broke the news to my mother, she looked deflated and wouldn't look me in the eye. I placed my hand on her small shoulder and tried to reassure her.

"It would only be for two years, Mom. And I'll be back for visits."

She sat there in silence, picking away at the corner of the placemat. Finally she said, "Who's going to be here for me if I need someone?"

I reassured her that my brothers would be here for her, "And you have a lot of dear friends here who adore you."

She nodded slightly and sighed, "But there's something about a daughter."

The lump in my throat choked me as I watched her struggle with the news, and the old doubts crept in again. Was I being selfish? Are we doing the right thing? But in the back of my mind, and deep in my heart, I knew there was a bigger story unfolding than just two Americans deciding to move to Crete on a whim.

We arrived on Crete on a hot August day in 2009, during the season when the island hums with the buzz of a billion cicadas and the heat drives locals and tourists alike to the cool waters of the sea. When my husband and I decided to pick up our lives and relocate to a Mediterranean island, my idea of what to expect was vague at best. We were both old enough to be settled into our careers but still young enough to embrace change. Only married for two years, we were still navigating the difficult territory of yours, mine, and ours that is inevitable with second marriages. Your car, my car, your house, my house, your kids, my kids, your friends, my friends, your cats, my dogs. We wanted to grasp onto something that was totally, unconditionally *ours*. Moving abroad was an opportunity to go out into the unknown hand in hand and make it *our* adventure, *our* life, *our* mess . . . together. And at times, it *was* messy . . . very messy. Brilliantly messy.

Crete's roots yield a slightly different fruit nurtured by the ebb and flow of seasons that define the essence of its culture. Because of the importance of seasons in the Greek culture, I have divided this book into seasonal sections, each one depicting not only the events that define a particular season but also the deeper soul changes that are inevitable with any expat. Every season has its ups and downs.

> With spring comes rain . . . and rejuvenation.
> With summer comes heat . . . and transformation.
> With autumn comes labor. . . and harvest.
> With winter comes darkness . . . and restful slumber.

During the time we lived on Crete, I kept a personal journal and published a photo blog. They included soul-searching entries, reflective musings, and even emotional tirades. Some of these entries are interspersed in italics throughout the book in an attempt to give the reader a close-up, timely view of events and people that shaped my personal journey.

Crazy, chaotic and captivating – Crete is an island like no other; knit together by family, faith, and food. A part of Greece, yet apart from Greece. Separated by a vast expanse of Mediterranean Sea from its mother country, Crete stands on its own with its feet firmly planted in a culture that has evolved over 5,000 years. The centuries of unwelcome foreign occupation only strengthened the fiercely independent spirit of its people. This independence is exhibited in the dance, stories, food, and traditions that are exclusive to the island. Crete holds to its own traditions with stubborn determination, and takes a certain pride in being dubbed the "bastard hillbilly child" of mainland Greece.

Cretans are a tough group of survivalists with a creative bent. They have to be in order to eke out a living on this land; its very landscape requires a tough hand to tame it.

The Cretan hills are harsh and foreboding, accented by sheer cliffs and deep gorges. But the thousands of olive groves that dot the landscape in the shadows of the mountains are proof that the fertile soil produces abundant agricultural crops. Many of the local Greeks own small farms, and their gardens produce a variety of vegetables and fruits in such plenty that what the families don't consume, they sell at the local farmers' markets. This time of year, the olives are plumping up, the grapevines are heavy with fruit and sweet melons peek out from beneath their giant vines.

At first blush, Crete seems stuck in time. Change comes slowly to the island. But it does come, as sure as the winter waves that undulate on its rocky shores; as sure as the seasons that nurture the island culture. The Greek philosopher Heraclitus of Ephesus said, "Everything changes and nothing stands still. The road uphill and the road downhill are one and the same." Circumstances in our life take on different meaning depending on how we see them. Different people can travel the same road and see completely different views. Or as my mother used to say, "Life isn't what happens to you. It's what you DO with what happens to you."

Our five years in Crete was a testimony to this quote, and our hasty exit from the island was the culmination of bittersweet goodbyes to the island after a heartbreaking event that caused us to return home to the States. But we didn't leave empty-handed. Our hearts were full and our lives changed in ways unimaginable. Ways that would be invaluable in helping us meet the challenges ahead with grace and strength. Living in Crete as a foreigner was a lesson in adapting to the unpredictable. We never knew what joys or struggles waited for us just around the corner. But one thing is certain . . . you can't come to Crete and leave unchanged.

This book is not intended to be a comprehensive travel guide, although I hope it will pique your interest to search out many of the fascinating places I mention. Nor is it intended to be a conclusive reference on the history of Crete. Crete's culture is multi-faceted and deeply layered, like a lovingly prepared Greek *moussaka* casserole.

Volumes of well-researched archeological findings have been written about Crete as the "center of western civilization" with thousands of years of history packed onto an island roughly 160 miles long and 40 miles wide. Even then, one gets the impression that there are still mysteries to be revealed in its ancient landscapes and rugged people.

The Greek word *meraki* describes the soul, creativity, or love put into something; the essence of yourself that is put into your work. I discovered meraki on the island of Crete, and have attempted to infuse it into every page of this book. My greatest hope is to convey my observations of this magical island in all its wackiness and wonder; this island that has the power to break, to change, to reinvent.

Which is exactly what it did to me.

SEEDLINGS

Though I do not believe that a plant will spring up
where no seed has been,
I have great faith in a seed. . .
Convince me that you have a seed there,
and I am prepared to expect wonders.

What lies behind us and what lies ahead of us
are tiny matters compared with
what lives within us.

—Henry David Thoreau

PINCH ME (PUNCH ME) — I LIVE HERE!

I looked through the foggy window of the airplane down to the great expanse of the Mediterranean Sea. In the distance, I could barely make out a sliver of land.

Crete. Our new home.

It had been a long journey already, starting with a cross-continental drive from the mountains of Colorado to the Eastern shore of Maryland. After leaving our car on the slow boat to Greece, we boarded a plane to continue our journey to the other side of the world. The long trip started with mind-numbing details followed by plenty of time to ponder over questions that loomed before me.

"How's my family back home?"

"Did I remember everything?"

"What time is it?"

"What DAY is it?"

"What have we done?" my husband's whisper interrupted my daydreaming. I looked at him, and to my surprise, witnessed a hint of incredulous shock. He looked past me out the window at the dry, weed-covered field where our plane was landing. A small terminal in need of updating and two cement runways welcomed us to the Hania International Airport. In the distance, small white-washed homes clung to the treeless hillside amidst the red and dusty earth. In fact, at first glance, red, brown and white were the predominant colors of Crete. I strained to look over the horizon to reassure myself that the beauty of the turquoise sea was still there.

We exited the plane into the glaring heat of the Greek summer sunshine and stepped down the passenger stairs. *There's no turning back now*, I thought. Nor did I want to. A new rush of adrenaline pulsed inside of me in spite of the bone-tiring jet lag. A flight attendant guided us into a shuttle full of passengers, mostly Greeks, and we were keenly aware of how it felt to be a minority. The shuttle bounced its way along the uneven pavement to the terminal. As we entered the doors of the terminal, the first thing I noticed was the complete lack of ventilation. The air was still, stifling, and stuffy, as though all the oxygen had been sucked out of the building.

The terminal itself was functional without any attention to fancy architectural touches. . . or air conditioning. I made a beeline for the nearest bathroom and squeezed into a cramped stall in the ladies room. It was there that I had my first lesson on Greek plumbing. A small sign above the toilet demanded, "Do not put paper down the toilet. Use the bin." I stifled a laugh when I realized it wasn't a joke. I knew this was the beginning of a long initiation into a world outside of my comfort zone. Something told me it was time to put away my snobbish American expectations and go with the flow.

Back in the baggage claim, Richard and I piled our luggage on a cart, and followed the crowd out to the main terminal where we joined other travelers searching for family and friends. We scanned the crowd for our sponsor from the US Navy base. She was easy to spot. A freckle-faced, red-headed American woman among the throng of black-haired, black-eyed, and mostly black-clad Greeks. The locals greeted family and friends with huge hugs and lots of noise. Our sponsor Deb, flashed a warm smile at us, gave us both a hug and said, "Welcome to Crete!"

To my surprise, her car was parked unapologetically in front at the curb along with dozens of others in a chaotic display of temporary parking. Somehow, we managed to stuff our entire collection of luggage into her small car and soon we bumped along the road out of the airport, passing rustic homes, warehouses, and farms. As we curved around through the dry, harsh landscape of the Akrotiri Peninsula I heard Richard whisper again, "What have we done?" I fought back the urge to echo him. Instead, I lightheartedly remarked, "We moved to a Mediterranean island and it's an adventure, remember?"

The postcard images of Santorini faded. I thought to myself, *It looks more like Mexico, with olive trees instead of cacti.*

The rural setting was dotted with ramshackle huts, many of which were in a state of perpetual construction with the tired look of surrender. To my surprise, the only trees visible were short gnarly olive trees and the occasional eucalyptus. As the car jerked around to avoid the inevitable potholes, I noticed that most of the small farms sported makeshift shelters for the equally worn-out looking livestock, which included chickens, goats, and the ugliest sheep I'd ever seen. But always before us was that beautiful, shimmering sea. Our hosts chatted on about the benefits of living on Crete while we tried to absorb it all.

A large, rusty chain-linked fence came into view as we approached the village of Horafakia. Dozens of paint-chipped mailboxes in varying shades of faded colors hung on the fence like a giant conglomeration of modern metal art. When we questioned Deb, she casually answered with a wink to her spouse, "Oh, that's the village post office. No one has mailing addresses so they all just pick up their mail here."

As we drove into Horafakia all apprehension faded away. The little village church was well tended to, its terrace and walls scrubbed clean, the shutters and the door freshly painted. Simple white-washed houses crowded the edges of narrow road. Flowers and herbs bursting with colors and scents filled the tiny yards behind low stone walls. Large covered terraces adorned with potted flowers held ample seating for outdoor living and dining.

I was completely charmed by the simplicity of it, and something I couldn't describe resonated with me. *I could live here*, I thought. *I DO live here.* In my very American touristy voice, I chirped, "Oh, how sweet!" But as I glanced over to my husband for affirmation, I could see the "charm" of it all was lost on my engineer/architect-German-bred I-just-want-trains-and-bike-lanes city boy. And I thought to myself, *Oooo, It's going to be a long two years.*

But I also knew Richard embodied the soul of an eternal optimist in the skin of an adventurer. And here was adventure staring us in the face with a dare and a promise: *Will you step out of your American skin long enough to observe and absorb? If you will, you will be changed forever.*

FIRST IMPRESSIONS

"We're not in Kansas anymore, Toto"
—Dorothy Gale, The Wizard of Oz

Dear family and friends,

I'm writing this email from a rather dull looking computer room at the Souda Bay Naval Base, our little piece of America for the next couple of years on this wild and wonderful island. Our move here was mostly uneventful but I'm still finding it hard to grasp the decision we've made to live abroad. My feelings of excitement tempered with doubts all contribute to the surreal wonder of it all. I keep reminding myself, Crete is our HOME now, at least for a while.

Specifically, home is on the Akrotiri Peninsula, a rural area of northwest Crete dotted with small family farms and olive groves. These disheveled little farms, complete with goats, roosters, farm dogs, and all their cacophony of noise, surround us, as well as a chaotic infrastructure of potholed roads, unfinished buildings, and "island beater" cars. But this same area is also the one that produces abundant supplies of fresh produce, open skies, and simple hospitality.

And surrounding all of its wonder and warts is the beautiful Mediterranean Sea. Early fall is the perfect time of year because most of the tourists have exited and the water is deliciously warm. On most days, the sea has no significant tides, no waves, no sharks, and no jellyfish; just a wide-open aqua blue expanse that melts into the Mediterranean horizon like a pool of silk.

My first swim in the Aegean Sea is a vivid memory of immersion in transparent, cerulean liquid with hints of summer warmth still lingering. The sea floor had sandy patches nestled between volcanic rocks softened with carpets of velvety seaweed. Conversely, the shoreline was hard and unforgiving.

Jagged volcanic rock made it hard to find a comfortable place to sit, but I finally nestled into a smooth place with the sun at my back and a view toward the city of Hania. On this serene morning, I found my quiet place to get away, write, pray, and bask in the gentle sunlight. I say "gentle" because it seemed more muted than the piercing, clear light from the Colorado sun. Only a week ago we were in the mountains in the middle of America, and now we were here on an island in the middle of the Mediterranean Sea. I continued my letter home with my first impressions:

Our morning walks to the local cafe in Horafakia for coffee reveal something different every day. We pass simple stone houses, their gardens overflowing with flowers of every color. Roses, clematis, lantana, zinnia and other exotic flora grow like weeds out of the brown earth. A big heavy-laden pomegranate tree hangs over the narrow road through the village. As we open the door to the corner cafe, a waft of coffee and cigarette smoke greets us. We order up two Cafe Elinikos (Greek coffee) and my request for cream draws stares from the barista. I soon discovered, you should never stir Greek coffee unless you want to chew it instead of drink it.

Later that week, we ventured down to a local *taverna* (café/restaurant) for dinner. The Sunset Taverna was owned and operated by Maria, who had a reputation in the area for creating culinary magic. The night was mild, with a lovely breeze coming in from the north, so we sat on a short stone wall and took in the view over the Aegean water towards the old Venetian port city of Hania. The sunset over the sea exploded into a spectacular sky painting. We lingered there in silence, not wanting to break the spell of magic playing out before us over the water. But the enticing smells coming from the Sunset Taverna behind us jolted our senses, and we laughed as both our stomachs growled in unison. We hurried up the taverna's crooked stone steps and sat at a corner table under the grapevine-shaded portico. A young waiter named Manolis greeted us and spoke in perfect English.

"Kalispera. Hello. Would you like to come and choose your dinner?"

As is the norm in Crete, he invited us into the kitchen to choose our meal from the pots on the stove rather than from a menu. As he opened each pot, the aromas of oregano, wine, garlic, and various meats were enough to make our stomachs rumble for a sampling of everything. We finally decided on the lamb *kleftiko* (lamb slow-baked in parchment paper), stuffed peppers and tomatoes, a slice of Maria's signature mushroom pie, and a fresh authentic Greek salad (cucumbers, tomatoes, red onions, olives and feta—*no* lettuce.).

Returning to our table, we munched on a starter of *tzatziki* (cucumber-yogurt dip) and fresh-baked village bread. The eye-popping bougainvillea flowers behind me swayed in the gentle breeze as the huge red sun melting into the Aegean Sea bathed everything in its rosy light. The sounds of Crete were all around us in the tinkling of bells from a local goatherd and an occasional mew from one of the kittens playing at our feet. The fresh food, friendly conversation, and stellar views from the vine-covered terrace were mesmerizing. Life was as slow and smooth as the white wine we sipped; which was a blessing considering the challenges we were in for in the next few weeks and months.

The culture on this island is very laid back. NO ONE is in a hurry to do anything and rules are made for stretching. This could drive an efficient, type-A American over the edge unless he/she determines to adapt. Our favorite phrase these days is, "Crete is Crete!" No amount of complaining, arguing, whining, or pleading is going to change anything. So you might as well take a deep breath and enjoy it for what it is—a good word of advice for anyone who is thinking of traveling or living abroad. Actually, it can be very entertaining and charming once we step outside of our uptight, on time, stressed out, American skin.

Everything about those first few months in Crete had the excitement of adventure and the aroma of the exotic. Knowing that two years would hardly be enough to take it all in, I hit the ground running each morning. I've heard that one of the best ways to keep your brain in good working order and avoid middle-age mind atrophy is to shake things up a bit in your life—learn a new language, travel to somewhere unfamiliar, take up a new hobby or activity, widen your social circles to include people from diverse backgrounds. We were bombarded with all that and more as we navigated the unfamiliar waters of US military protocol and culture shock in Greece.

I set off on a personal quest to immerse myself in this new culture at all costs. And sometimes, most times, that cost was my pride. I learned very quickly the nuances of Greek life in Crete simply by observing and inquiring. When you are a visitor in a foreign land, it's advisable to ease into your surroundings by keeping your eyes open and your mouth shut. Americans have the reputation abroad as being friendly, helpful, and happy, but also loud, naïve, and insensitive. But the truth is, the sooner one realizes that it's better to try to fit in, the more relaxed and accepting everyone is.

This is our first week here, and I still can't believe we've moved to this island to LIVE. I find that words escape me when I try to describe even this little part of Crete except in generic terms that paint a postcard picture. But that only scratches the surface of this mysterious place. I can only say it is beautifully rugged, backward, casual, dry, serene, yet with a certain intensity about it I've yet to discover. My quest for the next two years is to be able to nail down the "essence" of this place—the music of its soul, all the crescendos and staccatos that that give meaning to its song.

LOST IN TRANSLATION

"Poetry is what is lost in translation"

—Robert Frost

"It's Greek to me."

Until I moved to Greece, I couldn't fully grasp the real significance of that common phrase. Greek ranks up there with the most difficult languages to learn because its roots are not Latin. They are, well . . . Greek, of course. So it's not even remotely close to English. Think LONG words with usually four or more syllables. Not only does it sound unusual, it is very difficult to wrap your tongue around words that taste so unfamiliar.

When I first arrived on the island, I opened a blank journal that a friend gave me and proceeded to make lists on the first few pages. It was my Mediterranean/European Bucket List and it was full to the brim.

    1. Places to explore on Crete
        (Beaches, villages, mountains, archeological sites, cultural curiosities)

2. Places to explore beyond Crete
   (ten countries, thirty cities)
3. Experiences NOT to miss on the island!
   (Farmers' markets, harvests, Greek wedding, Orthodox
   Easter, sea kayaking, cooking lessons, *learn simple
   Greek*)

That last one makes me laugh now in hindsight. How naïve I was to think that any part of the Greek language was simple. Actually, I picked up the alphabet fairly quickly, but reading the words is a far cry from understanding their meaning. I confess that I blundered through many conversations when I refused to speak English and instead put my Greek to the test. This stubbornness usually resulted in my embarrassment to the delight and entertainment of others.

Take, for instance, my first trip to the Greek butcher. On my way to the village of Kounipidiana (case in point: *Koo-noo-pee-dee-a-na*), I practiced over and over the phrase requesting a whole chicken to roast (minus the head and feet). When I arrived at the butcher, the conversation went something like this:

Me: *Tha ithela ena kotopolo* (I would like a chicken) *horis to kefali kai horis pedia, parakalo* (without head and without feet, please).
Butcher: *Ti??* (What??)
Me: (repeated first phrase – a little slooooower and LOUDER)

Butcher: (chuckling and calling to his friend in the back) Gianni!

Butcher #2 (to me): *Ti thelete?* (What do you want?)

Me: (repeated same phrase louder with exaggerated hand motions) Cut off head and feet, please!

Both butchers laughed and said something in Greek as one grabbed a chicken, hacked off the head and feet, placed them in a package with the rest of the chicken and handed the whole mess to me. As I paid for my purchase, said thank you (*Efharisto*) and somewhat sheepishly exited the shop, I could still hear them laughing.

Later, I was telling a Greek-speaking British friend about my experience. When I told her what I'd said, she burst into laughter and said, "Well, you just asked the butcher for a chicken without a head and without *children!*" Turns out the word for feet is *po-DI-a* and the word for children is *PE-dia*. Details.

But by far, the most embarrassing exchange was when I stopped to buy some fresh vegetables from a local roadside stand. It was early spring and the seasonal produce included winter vegetables like cabbage, beans, cauliflower, and carrots. No tomatoes, and definitely no cucumbers. While making my choices I noticed the farmer's little boy shyly looking up at me. In an attempt at polite conversation, I remarked to the father in my best Greek, "Your little boy is very nice." He looked at me with a funny expression, smiled and actually blushed. Let me just say that the word for *boy* is only one letter off from the word for *cucumber*. What a difference one letter makes. I think he was actually flattered and probably went home that night and bragged to his wife, "That crazy American lady thinks I have a nice cucumber."

And sometimes even in speaking English there are possibilities for misconceptions because of thick accents. Sotiris, our Greek liaison from the Navy base, was interpreting for us as we met with our new landlords to seal the deal on our permanent rental home. After the process of meeting and greeting, answering questions and finally signing papers, Sotiris handed us a couple sets of house keys and said in his heavy Greek accent, "Now you have to kiss." For an awkward moment I was anxiously trying to decipher what this exactly meant—*Now we have to kiss?? Is this a customary two-cheek peck to seal the deal?* But when no one else moved in that direction it hit me. What he actually said was, "Now you have two *keys*." Relief!

Lost in translation moments were funny, exasperating, memorable, and mostly humbling. But I discovered that if we look past what separates us and instead focus on what makes us similar, the cream rises to the top and we find the sweetest of the fare. Universal kinships usually stem from the simple things like music, food, children, and laughter. I've seen even the gruffest of faces light up when you catch their eye and be the first to smile. We've been invited to strangers' tables to sample unusual food and strong drink, and immediate connections have been sparked by taking the time to admire a baby in her mother's arms or by sharing a laugh over a humorous scene playing out in the village square. And being a musician, I found many opportunities to share a song or two whenever the urge hit me or whenever it was needed.

Villa Kerasia B&B near Heraklion, Crete, was the location of many long dinners, great conversations, and lively entertainment. It quickly became one of our favorite getaways close to home and it was there that we met Mixalis (Mike), an older Greek gentleman with a penchant for yoga (three hours a day) and a passion for music. He was delighted when I showed up with my guitar in tow and we sang and played for two hours as other guests joined in.

"Mike, would you teach me a Greek song?" I finally asked him.

"Of course," he said. I will show you the most beautiful love song. Very popular in Crete."

And he proceeded to sing the hauntingly beautiful folk song, *S'agapo*. He wrote down the words and chords on a scrap piece of paper and handed them to me. Before he let go of the paper, he looked me straight in the eye and said, "Now, you must teach me an American song."

"Sure! " I agreed. "Anything in particular you want to learn?"

I wasn't prepared for his answer.

"Anything by Elvis!" he responded with excitement.

I imagine that somewhere in Greece right now, there is a lovely old man playing his banged-up guitar and crooning out *Love Me Tender* in a heavy Greek accent.

My most satisfying experience with sharing music was giving guitar lessons in our home city of Hania, Crete. Two girls in particular, Christina and Stavroula, were best friends and typical exuberant teens looking for more contemporary music than they could learn in their Greek music programs. In other words, they wanted to learn anything by Taylor Swift. We all looked forward to our weekly sessions and even included some line dancing to round out our Country Western experience. After years of lessons, expanded friendships with their families, and multiple shared events, these girls continue to be shining stars in my life; all because we shared a love of music.

But my most precious musical memory is from our little church in Hania. The tiny congregation, composed of mostly Greeks and Bulgarians with a smattering of English speakers, gathered every Sunday morning in a simple one-room space that served as a chapel on a back street in the heart of the city. Most Sundays, faithful congregants and curious visitors filled the old wooden pews as the service began with singing. Many of the songs were old familiar hymns led by Tania on vocals and accompanied by her husband, Haris, on a small keyboard. I still smile when I remember the annoying drum machine function that bolstered every song. These sweet Bulgarians didn't speak a lick of English, but when they led us in worship, the entire church sang with unbridled fervor in their native tongue. Believe me, there is something otherworldly and divine about hearing a hymn sung in different languages but in perfect harmony as a family lifting up praises to our Father.

Whether it was a hospital or old folks home in Hania or a private party or an old church, no one ever turned me down when I asked, "May I share a song with you?" And every time, without exception, I was rewarded with a smile and a thank you full of gratitude and emotion. It didn't even matter if I sang an unfamiliar tune in English, what mattered was that I shared a gift with people.

I am reminded that whenever and wherever we travel, we are ambassadors of good will from our home country and it's always a good idea to bring a gift to your hosts. Like no other offering, the gift of music has the power to translate meanings that are deeper than words and transform strangers into friends.

AUTUMN

All across the Mediterranean, the dance of the harvest begins as locals everywhere anticipate the gathering of grapes and olives. Countless generations for centuries before them joined in this dance. And Crete is no different. This is the season for gathering in; the season for reaping all that was sown. Long days and hard work meant a bountiful harvest.

When autumn arrives, the oppressive heat of summer departs and takes with it the crowds of tourists reddened and subdued by the Mediterranean sun and sea. At their exit, every living thing on the island seems to breathe a collective sigh of relief. The tavernas are filled with mostly locals, lingering longer over their meals and swapping stories of summer past. The summer song of the cicadas is replaced by the whirring of the harvester rods in the olive trees.

We discovered this was the best time for being outdoors. Milder temps, warm water, and fewer people made for the perfect hike, bike, swim, or road trip. Autumn was our season of gathering in - not grapes or olives, but stories and experiences to savor over the coming winter months. Grapes and olives—sweet and salty, much like our lives were becoming. We didn't have the foggiest idea what we were in for, but we knew we would probably be in a state of perpetual surprise. How right we were.

HOME SWEET CRETE HOME

What we call the end is also a beginning.
The end is where we start from.

—T. S. Eliot

We arrived on the island with two large suitcases, one guitar and a million questions. *Where will we live? How can we get a rental car? When will our own car arrive? When will the rest of our belongings arrive? How do we find a church? Will Richard like his job and colleagues?*

Where's the nearest coffee shop?

Thankfully, Deb, our sponsor from the base, had already taken care of many of those items on our list. She secured a temporary place to live, even stocked the refrigerator with a few essentials, helped us find a rental car and answered questions about our belongings. Finding a church and a good coffee shop would be up to us. In the meantime, we took our two suitcases and my guitar and settled in as best we could to our temporary digs.

Our apartment was in a village called Stavros, located at the end of the Akrotiri Peninsula. Two entertaining and big-hearted Brits, Daphne and Reg, managed the resort complex. Thanks to their hospitality and knowledge of the island, they significantly softened and enriched our initiation into this new culture. Reg and I shared a love for guitars and music, and many nights we enjoyed live music (accompanied by great food and ample drink) with international guests and close neighbors who shared the same interests. Our poolside parties usually included Daphne's mouth-watering slow-roasted chicken and potatoes along with traditional Greek salad and *tsatsiki dip* and as the night wore on the music got better . . . or maybe the drinks got better. Either way, it was always a good time for folks to gather and enjoy the mild evenings together under the swaying palm trees by the pool.

Truth be told, the best thing about the Artemis was Daphne and Reg, certainly not the accommodations that were typical Cretan rustic. Instead of chairs and a sofa, the living space was arranged with two cement "day bed" platforms covered with an upholstered 2-inch foam piece. If we wanted to watch the little TV perched high on a corner shelf, we had to move the uncomfortable straight-backed taverna chairs into view. No problem, since all the TV stations were Greek and other more important dilemmas needed our attention—like how to stop the sideways rain from blowing in under the closed window and soaking my computer keyboard. But what we lacked in accommodations, Reg and Daph compensated for in their friendship, so when we finally found our permanent home, our parting was bittersweet.

One quiet October evening, Richard and I walked from the Artemis down to the sea at Stavros Cove. The beach was empty except for a sole wanderer and a couple of stray dogs frolicking in the sand. The setting sun played off the red cliffs of Stavros, reflecting their barren faces in the water that was as still as the sky above. We walked barefoot at the water's edge until dusk settled into darkness and the stars appeared. Returning home after dark, we sat outside, soaking up the balmy breeze and laughing at the kittens chasing bugs under the lamplight. Gratitude welled up inside me for that moment, that time, that place. And as time passed, I had much more to be thankful for.

After about three months of living in Crete, little by little, pieces of home started arriving. We picked up our car from the ferry port and shortly afterwards our main shipment of furniture, including my piano, arrived just in time to settle in to our new home. Our permanent home was located outside the small village of Horafakia, which means "little farmlands," a perfect description of the landscape. The two-story house sat in the middle of a small olive grove surrounded by a high stone wall.

Perched on a rise above the countryside, we enjoyed loads of sunshine and cooling sea breezes. The expansive views opened full circle from the loft terrace upstairs. To the north we could gaze over vineyards and olive groves out to the Aegean Sea and to the south the mountains of the impressive *Lefka Ori* (White Mountain) range loomed above the city of Hania. The west view promised beautiful sunsets over the sea and the Rodoupou Peninsula beyond. The big dining room window on the east side of the house framed a distant monastery surrounded by more fields and farmlands that gently nestled in under the cliffs of Stavros. The late afternoon Mediterranean sun reflecting off the cliffs seemed to set them on fire; the red orb painting its last brilliant glow on their faces before setting into the sea.

We spent many an evening on the rooftop terrace with a glass of wine, a slab of feta drizzled with olive oil, and plate of seasonal fruit. Sometimes we talked about our day. Other times, we simply lounged in silence as the sun set and the first stars of the night appeared. This was our distant view. But just to keep it real, next to us in a vacant lot stood a fully occupied pigsty and an old broken-down late-model rusted-out car covered in weeds. We quickly discovered it's all part of the Crete experience. Just when you think you've seen it all, something else turns up to surprise, delight, or shock you; like Greek driving habits.

Driving down into the city of Hania for the first time was challenging at best as we set out on a Saturday morning to find the farmer's market located in the center of the city. We navigated our little (by American standards) Honda sedan through the congested, narrow streets of Hania while desperately trying not to succumb to hair-pulling frustration due to close encounters with Greek drivers. As we rounded a corner, we came up behind a car stopped cold in the middle of the street with its hazard lights flashing. The occupant of the car opened the door and slowly meandered over to a nearby mini-mart. As cars started backing up behind us in a long line on this busy Saturday morning, I gently tooted the horn but was only met with a blank stare. A few minutes later, the driver came out of the mini-mart with a cold frappe drink and a pack of cigarettes. Oblivious to the traffic knotted up behind him, he got back in his car and zoomed off.

I'm convinced the Greeks invented the automobile hazard light. They use it boldly and frequently. The car itself might be a run-down, broken-down, rusted-out piece of metal on four bald tires, but you can be certain the hazard lights are in full working order. I soon found out that what I considered rude was simply a common occurrence and part of the culture of chaos on Crete. But the most astonishing thing was that nobody seemed to mind. Everyone either slowly maneuvered around him or just waited patiently as traffic backed up behind him until he returned and sped off down the road. No angry blasts of the horns, no loud yelling accompanied by clenched fists, and no finger salutes—quite refreshing, actually, if you can get past the aggravation.

When we finally made it to the city, we faced another challenge: parking. Finding a place at a car park was fruitless, so we reverted to street parking. The side streets in Hania were packed. Every turn revealed a conglomeration of one-way passages barely wide enough for one car. Cars nestled into any space they could squeeze into—front, back, or sideways, taking out a major section of sidewalk. In a crowded city of 70,000 inhabitants, it appeared to be a type of survival of the fittest, or more correctly, opportunist. We weaved our way slowly between precariously parked cars and finally squeezed into a space. As we hesitantly walked away from our car, we wondered how many new scratches or dents we would come back to.

When most people heard we moved to a Mediterranean island for two years, there was a mix of envy and incredulous curiosity. In their mind's eye, many saw only the sunny beaches and blue domed roofs of the typical Greek postcard; very glamorous indeed, but not the whole story. Vacationing here is one thing; living here is a whole different story. As with any culture, there are the nuts and bolts, the yin and yang, the nitty-gritty details that tell what it's really all about—a whole Shakespearean comedy/tragedy.

I admit there were days when I wondered, *What have we done?!* Those days when the electric company decided to go on strike (again) and the power was off for hours, or the internet was down for weeks, and those sleepless nights due to the continuous cacophony of dogs and roosters. The consecutive winter days of nerve-racking winds that drove the rain sideways challenged my sanity, and the sight of pathetic-looking stray cats and dogs broke my heart. But worst of all was the overwhelming feeling of isolation and loneliness. On those days I found solace by immersing myself in prayer and reading . . . and writing about it all.

The unpredictable autumn weather reminded me that everything has its season. After days of rain and gloom, the sun would reappear, maybe even accompanied with a glorious rainbow over the sea, and I would receive the gift of seeing with my eyes, not just my heart, the beauty of all that God gives: blue sky, silken sea, and gentle breezes; fragrant thyme from the hills, warm clear air, and soft bleating from nearby sheep.

God weaves the ugly into the heavenly and creates a masterpiece with his fingerprints all over it. Things aren't always as they seem and a masterpiece takes time. So it is with our lives.

Every tapestry includes a rough underside of confusing stitches and unruly knots lovingly fashioned by the master's hand. The pattern seems to have no rhyme or reason, just a puzzling entanglement of threads and a random array of color.

The question rises up inside us, *How can anything beautiful come out of that mess?* But turn it over and the truth about us, his masterpiece, is revealed in a life created by and for beauty. Every stitch has its purpose for the bigger picture. A magnificent life is not the result of quick, easy paint-by-number perfection, but rather it is borne out of the wreckage of a million knots and stitches of tragedy, persistence and hope guided by the skillful hand of a loving Father.

Tragedy, persistence, hope—these things became my companions through a deeply traumatic event years later, and looking back, I could see that the time spent in Crete tested and taught me in preparation. For now, I was still learning how find balance in a country that felt off- balance. To understand a culture, we first have to look at its history, a tapestry of events stitched with the colors of tears and triumphs. Crete's history told through stories passed down through the generations and whispered in the silent halls of the island's old monasteries.

THREE MONASTERIES AND A SMILING MONK

I can see the domed top of Agia Triada Monastery from my dining room window. It sits in the shadow of the Stavros hills, surrounded by grapevines and olive groves. The late afternoon sun illuminates the monastery, and it looks like a golden ark floating on a sea of blue-green olive trees. Mesmerizing.

One sunny autumn morning, we jumped on our bikes and peddled out from our house on the rural road that meandered through fields of fragrant wild oregano and thyme. The autumn-brown dusty earth beneath the olive groves had been transformed into a plush carpet of bright green clover thanks to the early and abundant winter rains. As we neared Agia Triada Monastery, the road became straight, lined with rows of giant eucalyptus trees and long stone walls that looked as if they had grown up together over the decades. The Mediterranean sun cast its glow over the coppery stones that had been hewn out of the rich, red Akrotiri soil.

We pedaled down the lane under a shadowy canopy of eucalyptus branches that spread high above their whitewashed trunks. In the distance, at the end of the lane, we could see the wide stone steps that led up to the monastery. It was a crisp autumn day and the church's white bell tower stood out in contrast against the deep blue sky reminding me of the colors in the classic Greek flag. Morning was a good time to visit the monastery, before the old immense doors were closed for the afternoon siesta.

There are, in fact, three monasteries, two still active, one in ruins, all with deep histories marking the long influence of Greek Orthodoxy on the island: *Agia Triada* (Holy Trinity), *Gouverneto Monastery* (Our Lady of the Angels), and the abandoned ruins of *Katholiko Monastery*. Much to our delight, they are all located on the Akrotiri within hiking/biking distance of each other.

We rested our bikes against the old stone staircase and climbed up the massive steps and into the open entrance of the monastery. The large inner courtyard was quiet with no sign of the five monks who lived within its original seventeenth-century walls. We sat on a bench in the courtyard sipping on our water bottles and sharing the sun with a dozen or so stray cats that had been adopted by the monks. During the summer, an unassuming monk sits at the entrance doors to collect a fee of a couple of euros and politely remind you that photos are strictly forbidden. Buses of tourists clamor inside the monastery to grab a bit of history and sneak a few photos before loading back on to the bus and rushing out to the next sightseeing stop. But this day, the monastery was an oasis of quiet. We discovered that the off-season is the best time to slow down and soak up the peace and beauty of this impressive place.

As I walked on the old stone pavers surrounding the whitewashed chapel, I imagined the two brothers, highly educated monks, whose vision was to build a sanctuary for education and religion that would become Agia Triada. I wondered if they ever imagined their monastery would eventually house a prestigious theological school and library complete with priceless Christian relics and manuscripts. And I shuddered to think about the Turkish raids on this peaceful place that resulted in the burning and destruction of those antiquities during the 1821 Greek Revolution. But some things are destined to rise out of the ashes. Today, Agia Triada still plays an important role in the religious and educational community of Crete and is considered a major historical monument.

Richard and I walked every nook and cranny of that old monastery courtyard, stepping over sleeping cats, wandering under porticos of flower-laden vines, and marveling over giant Greek pots almost as tall as me. Did they at one time hold precious stores of olive oil or wine produced by the monastery? We circled around again to the entrance and ascended up the stone steps to the bell tower that was perched on top of a high terrace above the main doors. We sat on the upper terrace with our backs against the warm stone wall and our legs stretched out in front of us, soaking up the sun and the silence. From our vantage point we could look over the expansive and prolific vineyards and olive groves tended to by the monks. The monastery was clearly responsible for more than just the spiritual nourishment of its community.

A monk calling up to us startled us out of our quiet repose on the wall. He motioned for us to come down as he rattled on in Greek glancing at his watch and pointing to the entrance. It was siesta time. He ushered us towards the entrance and with a final nod, closed the giant wood doors with a soft thud.

Not ready to head home, we decided to continue up the road towards the Gouverneto Monastery past old church ruins, neat rows of grapevines, a cluster of beehives, free-ranging goats, and up into a ravine where the road gave way to rough cement and steep curves. When we finally crested the hill and arrived at the monastery, we were tired and thirsty. We approached the garden gate and made our way up to Gouverneto, a humble monastery perched at the top of the mountain with views north over the endless Cretan Sea. Forgetting our thirst momentarily, we drank in the magnificent view from the crest of the hill. We noticed that the monastery doors were shut tight for siesta, so we ditched our bikes under a tree in the parking lot and hiked down to the ruins of Kathaliko Monastery.

Descending down a well-worn stone path, we soon stumbled upon an impressively large cavern with a small stone chapel carved out of the rock and filled with icons, candles, and the lingering smell of incense. Further into the cave there stood a rough stone altar and a pool of water that is still believed to be holy. In fact, many modern-day believers continue to make a pilgrimage to this cave at certain times of the year. St. John the Hermit was a frequent visitor to this holy site and lived in a cave farther down the ravine behind where the ruins of the Moni Katholiko now stand.

To reach Katholiko we continued following the stone path and soon found ourselves rapidly descending down a zigzagging stone stairway that hung on the side of the mountain. As we neared the bottom of the gorge, the ruins of Katholiko came into view. A stone archway, a few buildings, a cistern, and a wide "bridge to nowhere" were tucked into the high walls of the gorge. The afternoon shadows had descended on the deep gorge and the deserted monastery ruins seemed strangely mystical and eerie. I remembered a legend about Katholiko that claimed repeated raids by pirates from the nearby coast eventually caused the monks to abandon the site and relocate to a more secure site the top of the hill. An unsubstantiated story, but still intriguing and curious. I stood there wondering what the stones would say if they could talk. And would their echoes be heard bouncing off the gorge walls as easily as ours, even as we talked in hushed voices?

I hardly noticed the arduous climb back up to Gouverneto, imagining the past inhabitants and their lives in this remote area centuries ago. When we finally arrived back at Gouverneto, siesta time was over but we were ready for a long rest. We climbed the wide stone staircase leading up to the entrance and entered through its massive, time-worn doors. The stone portico beyond the doors opened up into a peaceful courtyard filled with orange trees, winter flowers, and countless cats sprawled out on the sun-warmed pavers. A couple of young friendly felines hesitantly sauntered up to us, their hunger for a soft warm lap overriding any fear of us. I noticed each one had an ear clipped, indicating they had been spayed or neutered, an uncommon sight in Crete.

All of these cats were strays that had the good fortune of ending up in a secure place with a group of compassionate monks. They were the minority. Most cats on Crete are riddled with disease or injury shortening their life span significantly. They most often live in or near the dumpsters where they forage for food and avoid humans. A wild sort of feral cat, they are not usually friendly, but nonetheless my heart would break every time I'd see a sickly cat or kitten perched on top of a dumpster, their eyes full of hunger, pain, or fear. Monastery cats are typically much better off and it did my heart good to see the healthy cats here at Agia Gouverneto.

We were resting in the tranquil courtyard, thankful that the road home was an easy downhill ride from here, when a young monk with kind eyes and an easy smile approached us. He greeted us warmly.

"Kalimera. I am Siluon. Where are you from?" he said in perfect English.

We introduced ourselves and added, "We're from America, but live in Horafakia now."

"Ahhh . . . . Welcome! Did you hike here?"

When we explained that we rode our bicycles he seemed impressed, or more correctly, baffled by the fact that we made the trek up to the monastery on our bicycles.

"All the way from Horafakia?!"

"Well, HE rode the whole way," I answered, pointing to my husband. "I took my bike for a little walk up the gorge so I could see the scenery at a slower pace."

The humor was lost in translation but he smiled and nodded.

"Wait here," he said as he excused himself and slipped inside through a small door behind us.

He returned a few minutes later with a tray of chocolate-covered dates and two glasses of cold water. Not used to such hospitality and friendliness from a monk to foreigners, we graciously accepted his offering and began a conversation. He had been living in Gouverneto for many years under the tutelage of an older monk. He invited us to sit in the common room as the late afternoon became chilly and we continued our conversation. As the shadows deepened in the austere but comfortable room, our conversation deepened as well. He spoke of the Eastern Orthodox faith, its origins, and traditions.

"Our faith is shaped by the early church saints. We believe that the Eastern Orthodox Church is the true faith, and we have preserved the traditions and doctrines from centuries ago back to the original apostles. Orthodoxy actually means "right believing."

He continued on and for a moment I felt the cultural gap between us closing. The three of us in that room were all members of a worldwide assembly of human souls searching for meaning, belonging and love on earth. A collection of beings of different color, texture and design that makes up the tapestry of humanity created by the Master's Hands. That is where our similarities begin . . . and end. Small things can lead to big differences. But with a little patience and tolerance, and a lot of grace perhaps we can shrink the gap between our differences.

And on this autumn day spent with a pleasant and unassuming monk, the little things like a bike ride, the golden autumn sun, a glass of cold water, and a new friendship made a big difference in our view of Crete. We left the smiling monk at the monastery doors, mounted our bicycles, and threaded our way down the hill past vineyards dripping with ripe green and purple fruit. With high hopes, we realized yet another reason to appreciate autumn in Crete – the much anticipated grape harvest.

SWEET HARVESTS
THE FRUIT OF THE VINE AND OF FRIENDSHIP

It's October, but it looks like spring. The rains have nourished the summer-parched land and it's green again. The clarion skies of summer are now decorated with clouds of all shapes and sizes. The water continues to be that ever-changing color of aqua, but it is more restless. The flowers and fruits are lush and abundant; the lambs are frisky; and there is a heightened sense of activity as the locals prepare for the agricultural highlights of the year: the olive and grape harvests. As I write this, the grapes are fermenting in their casks; the chestnuts are gathered, and the countryside is humming with the sound of olive harvester rods.

In October, the olives are still plumping up and heavy on the branches, but the grapes on the vines are ripe and ready for harvest. In every village this succulent fruit is picked, pressed, and prepared for fermentation. Each household in the country villages have their own version of "village wine," which is brownish in color and has the interesting sweet taste of something like watered down sherry. I never could develop a taste for it, but much preferred the deep reds and crisp whites from the lush valley wine region in the hills above Crete's capital city, Heraklion. However, when we were invited to an old-fashioned traditional grape stomping party hosted by our dear friend Katerina and her family, we jumped on it—or should I say, jumped IN it?

Katerina told us to meet at her Yiayia's (grandmother's) home in Sternes on the Akrotiri. When we arrived at the little stone house and garden, a buzz of activity greeted us. Men were tossing crates of plumb-purple grapes into a cement enclosure called a *patitiria* (wine press) common in the landscape of any Greek garden where the family makes their own wine. This structure looked like an aboveground empty swimming pool about 8' by 8' with thick walls of stone. A pipe extended through the bottom of one of the walls and sat above a shallow well where a wine barrel, topped with a simple kitchen strainer to catch the solids, was poised to collect the precious juices.

Nothing is wasted. After the vines are pruned, the old wood is used for the fireplace. Grape leaves are used for cooking delicious Greek *dolmades* (stuffed grape leaves), the fruit is eaten fresh or cooked in sugar for marmalade. But of course, the most desired result of the grape harvest is the wine. The seeds, stems, and grape peels aren't thrown away, but instead they are distilled to produce *tsikoudia,* or potent spirits consumed for centuries in this part of the Mediterranean and commonly known as *raki,* a.k.a. "Cretan moonshine" or "jet fuel," depending on the taste. There are many theories as to how this drink got its name, but my favorite has

Turkish roots. During the Turkish occupation of Crete, the name *raki* was given to the local drink, tsikoudia. *Arak* in Arabic means "sweat," and *araki* means "that which makes one sweat" – no joke, since it has a tendency to burn all the way down after the first swallow.

When we arrived at Yiayia's home, everything was set up and just waiting for some local labor. I timidly asked where I should first wash my feet, but was dismissed, and before I knew it, I was knee-deep in a concoction of squishy, slippery grapes and tender, pokey stems. Traditionally, the women did the stomping, and it was no different this day. About six of us, holding on to each other for support, picked up our skirts and stomped, squished, and laughed hysterically through the process of extracting juices from the deep purple grapes. As I looked over to my redheaded friend, a flashback of a grape-stomping scene from *The Lucy Show* came to mind and I remarked that all she needed was a bandana around her head.

Katerina's uncle kept supplying us with more grapes to smash, and her father gathered the large containers as they filled with juice and transported them to the wine cellar next to the garden. We were all in great spirits, probably due in part to the copious amounts of last year's fruit of the vine we consumed while working, but also simply because it was a beautiful day on the island to enjoy a new experience with new friends.

All this time, the other women of the family were busily preparing and laying a feast of Greek delights that could feed an army. The large table on the patio under the trees was dressed with a traditional Cretan white tablecloth, simple white porcelain plates, glass wine cups, an enormous bowl of grapes, a plate of Greek cookies, and glass carafes of wine, water, olive oil, and *tsikoudia*. And these were just the *mezedes* (starters)! As we finished up our work, we each crawled out of the patitiria, washed off our feet with a nearby hose, and padded barefoot over the warm stone path to the lunch table set with huge amounts of food. Lunch was a delectable array of rice pilaf, lamb, chicken, pork, dolmades, *horiatiki* (Greek salad) tzatziki dip, stuffed peppers and tomatoes, and crusty village bread. "More, please" is something you will never hear around a Greek table. Before you can even think it, the food appears and keeps on appearing, even after your stomach is pleading for mercy. Sitting under the shade of the trees and grape-laden vines of the pergola, we raised our glasses to the harvest, to the food, and especially to family and friends.

The Greek word for hospitality is *xenia*, the generosity and courtesy extended to strangers and friends alike who are in one's home. We were offered bounteous amounts of *xenia* in the years we lived on Crete. A couple of years later, we were invited to soak in more Cretan good cheer and companionship. We gathered at the home of Katerina's new husband's family in the mountain village of Vrisses and were served up a plentiful supply of Greek hospitality and delicious food. Katerina's husband, Sifis, went out of his way to insure we were spoiled and fully satisfied. His family welcomed us into their charming, traditional home that had all the warmth of a well lived-in family house, complete with their own Cretan family history tastefully displayed from floor to ceiling. The old structure, originally a storage room/stable dating back to the late eighteen hundreds, was lovingly renovated and decorated by Sifis's parents. The attention to detail inside and out was evident everywhere you looked. Katerina summed up the value of heritage when she said, "Given how important family is in Greece, maintaining and improving family property is like paying respect to your ancestors. This is why I believe this house is so close to Sifis' heart, and now mine, and I'm sure our kids will feel the same someday."

Our hosts served up a lunch of great magnitude in quality and quantity and made it look so easy in the process. As we took a "tour" of the museum-like home, Katerina and her mother-in-law put the finishing touches on the meal in the tiny kitchen. Sifis and his father entertained us with old family stories inspired by the photos and implements hanging on the old stone walls. It was hard to concentrate on the conversation as heavenly smells began to waft in from the succulent pork and chicken dish that was baking in the outdoor oven. Finally, we took our places at the long wooden table that filled the front room. We sampled and sipped our way through the afternoon, finishing the feast off with some delicious desserts, followed by shots of homemade tsikoudia infused with fig and honey. Sifis' family graciously embodied the concept of *xenia* that day, and we left feeling as though we had been guests of honor at an intimate Mediterranean family dinner.

As always, each gathering around a table included feasting on more than just food. A good story or two always unfolded – the most interesting being the reminiscent tales and legends told by the older generation. And that was perhaps the most interesting and sometimes astounding revelation we experienced as expats living on Crete: the generous mix of history, myth, and religion all blended into centuries of superstition, orthodoxy, and traditions that make Crete, uniquely Crete. It is truly, as Barry Unsworth says, "the quintessential land of such fusions." Nowhere was this phenomenon more evident than in the little villages tucked into the hills and hanging off the mountain slopes of inland Crete. When passing through these villages, preferably by foot or bike, it was often surprising to my foreign eyes to see the startling blend of neglect and nurture. The animals were skinny and mangy-looking; the roads were wrought with potholes; the houses were crumbling and the infrastructure was makeshift; but the patios were freshly washed; the clean laundry was hanging on the line; the vegetable gardens and orchards were carefully tended; and the chapels were pristine.

Barry Unsworth describes in his travel chronicle, _Crete_, a typical sight,

These village churches have an air of complete and utter tranquility. They are swept and clean, the beveled red roof tiles are repaired or replaced, the walls are whitewashed, there are well-tended gardens all around. Often enough you see no one, but the care of some hand is everywhere evident, a blend of the devotional and the domestic, cats and fig trees and icons all mixed in together. Never a formal garden, no sense of elaboration, no concept of dignifying the space around, but a gardener's care for plants for their own sake, and for what they might yield, the lemon, the fig, and the almond growing among trees planted only for their flowers or the beauty of their shape."

In other words, the only things under constant repair and close management seemed to be the kitchens and the chapels, each a testimony to the importance of family and church in this culture.

We are often asked the question, "How did living in Crete change you?" Patience, tolerance, and wonderful friendships were some of the most precious rewards. But the most treasured gift was that we learned to depend on God more and on things less. We all live in a world of constant, and sometimes frantic change, and Crete adds the element of unpredictability, so it can be exasperating at times. We survived those days by remembering two words: *breathe* and *pray*. And then reframe and look at things differently. We learned to not look too closely or judge too severely the anarchic surroundings. It's a much prettier sight when your gaze is focused on the serenity of larger vistas rather than the rubbish beneath your feet.

So, I wrap this quiet afternoon around me like an old familiar comforter and succumb to the sense of complete contentment. I find the most enjoyment in the simple things of God's creation. The autumn sky is defined by an array of clouds that are absent all summer; the pink-blossomed wild thyme bushes decorate the hillsides with a heady aroma; the dry brown earth under the olive trees has been replaced by a thick carpet of bright green clover; the sea is a deeper shade of blue; the beaches are empty; and the afternoon sun paints the cliffs of Stavros a brilliant shade of copper. In the distance, a herd of sheep follows its shepherd down from the hills and their soft tinkling of bells lulls me into a half sleep. And this scripture from the Psalms crosses my mind,

> *"If I rise on the wings of the dawn,*
> *If I settle on the far side of the sea,*
> *Even there your hand will guide me,*
> *Your right hand will hold me fast.*

(Psalm 139:9, 10)

THE CHESTNUT FESTIVAL

The Greek calendar is bulging with festivals celebrating everything from the religious to the frivolous, the ancient to the modern. The phrase "pulling out the stops" must have Greek origins, because when the Greeks throw a party, they do it on a grand scale. Not fancy-grand, stuffy, elegant, or posh, but instead, a joyously chaotic event full of food, music, laughter, and noise in quantities that cause your head to spin. It's a blissfully exhausting way to spend an unforgettable night.

Most visitors to Crete stay close to the water, which is understandable—the Mediterranean waters are one of the most beautiful sights on Earth, and the sea is just as integral to this culture as the mountains. But to experience the "real Crete," you must head inland and up into the mountain villages. Some summer visitors do just that, in an attempt to do something different to stay cool and return to their seaside hotel rooms with a new, and (I hope) an enlightened perspective. But my favorite time to explore these outward-bound destinations is during the shoulder seasons of fall and spring.

In October, the chestnut trees are in full dress, adorned with their bright green, spiny-covered fruit, clinging to hillsides and filling valleys with shade and sustenance for both animals and people. We headed into the hills one afternoon for the annual chestnut festival in Elos, a charming little mountain village about an hour from Hania. (A note about events: if you are dependent upon the internet to find dates and locations of specific seasonal events, you might be searching in vain. It's never a sure thing, even when it's supposed to be a sure thing. It's difficult to even pin down a local travel agency to get information about events in the mountains. They are more than happy to help you with "tourist" events but you will most likely see a blank stare accompanied by the "Greek shrug" if you are looking for anything with a more local flair.) When I finally telephoned a village taverna in Elos to inquire about their local chestnut festival, my conversation went something like this:

"*Kalimera*, Hello. I'm trying to find out some information about the upcoming chestnut festival there in your village."

Long pause . . . "No English."

Here I resorted to my pathetic version of Greek, but was actually happy to try it out.

"*Kastanos festival sta Elos?*" (Chestnut festival in Elos?)

Here the voice on the other end of the line launched into a long stream of Greek words at machine-gun speed, ending with the one word I did understand, "*Ndaksi?*" (OK?)

"Uhhh . . . *Nai, efharisto.*" (Yes, thank you)

I hung up not learning a thing except I shouldn't ask a question in Greek unless I was totally prepared to hear the answer . . . in Greek.

But not to be undone, I picked up the phone and called the only other taverna in town. I humbly asked first,

"Do you speak English," and was relieved to hear the young man say, "Yes."

Oh good, I thought, this will be easy.

Wrong.

"I'm calling to find out when the chestnut festival is scheduled in your village."

"Yes, chestnuts."

"Do you have a festival?"

"Yes, festival." (*Good, now we're getting somewhere.*)

"When is it?"

"Here in Elos."

"When?"

"In town square, in Elos. Not a big village. No problem." (Here is where I realized that he thought I was asking, "where," and for the life of me I couldn't remember the word for "when.")

So I responded, "*Simera* (today)? *Avrio* (tomorrow)?"

"*Oshi* (No)."

(So we've hit a wall and there is a big pause. Where to go from here?)

By some miracle, he understood finally what I was trying to ask and offered the following.

"You ask when is chestnut festival?" (YES! Now we are getting somewhere. Wrong again.) "Festival is this week. Maybe next week. Whenever chestnuts ripe."

Big pause on my end. "Uhhh . . . *Ndaksi. Efharisto.*" (OK. Thank you.)

Buggers!

Thankfully, I have a good friend who speaks fluent Greek, and she rounded up all the information I needed. On a dazzling October Sunday afternoon, five of us—our two best friends on the island, my son who was visiting from the States, and Richard and I—loaded into our little Honda and drove up towards the mountain village of Elos, south of the coastal city of Hania. As we ventured deeper into the hills of Crete, the landscape changed from dry barren Mediterranean earth to densely vegetated crevices and slopes. There was something comforting about the presence of these tall deciduous trees that looked almost out of place on an island mostly populated with scrubby short olive trees. Their height alone was an invitation to walk in the diffused light of their shade.

Oaks, chestnuts, plane trees all competed with local shrubbery for space along roadsides and in dry creek beds. Each October brings cooler temperatures along with the first of winter's welcome rains that miraculously green up the brown dusty earth of summer. While the rains encourage new green growth underfoot at lower elevations, the mountain trees celebrate this seasonal change by adorning themselves in browns, yellows, and the occasional muted reds. Every turn in the road brought a new picture of Crete in the autumn.

We knew we were getting close to Elos when suddenly the road was lined on both sides with parked cars allowing only a skinny pass-through wide enough for one car. We parked and joined the parade of people walking towards the village. As we neared the town square, we were greeted by the musical sounds of the lyra and the guitar, punctuated by the garish exclamations of the MC in a too-loud microphone. It was obvious that a party was happening here. The square was roped off, and greeters at an entrance table took our €25 "donation" fee (this was a fundraising event) and motioned us on towards long rows of tables and chairs. A stage had been set up for entertainment where the musicians were already in full swing. One young man was expertly bowing out a feverish melody on the lyra, a predominate three-stringed Cretan instrument similar to a violin but held in an upright position on the lap. The other musicians accompanied him on the bouzouki (a lute-like instrument of varying sizes and tones), the mandolin, the guitar, and a large hand-held drum.

At first blush, Cretan music seems to be a chaotic mixture of frenzied tones competing and colliding with one another. But if you listen long enough, you begin to appreciate the sophisticated metrical rhythms and unusual intonations that sound so foreign to the Western ear. Crete's version of folk/blues music is the *rebetiko,* born out of the working class' need to express daily life through music. Topics of love, poverty, social injustice, war, and freedom are covered in an array of tempos and moods. Whether it's the slow mournful rendition of a heroic ballad, or the frenetic intensity of a traditional dance piece, Cretan musicians proudly preserve hundreds of years of tradition, telling stories through their music of the joys and tragedies their culture has experienced through the ages. When Cretan music is paired with dance, these forms of expression are beautifully wedded together. The festival dances are performed in traditional Cretan costume, rich with color and embellished with an array of shiny ornaments.

We watched as the first group of female dancers approached the stage and formed a line, arms linked. The musicians started playing a slow folk song, and as they gradually increased the tempo, the dancers kept up with them, arms linked, tiptoeing circularly across the stage. Each dancer took turns breaking away from the group and moving center stage, she whirled, twisted, and dipped as her nimble feet stepped in time with the accelerating music. Their faces were etched with concentration. Their movements were graceful and intentional. A loud applause rose from the large audience as they finished their dance with an abrupt stomp of the foot and lift of the chin.

The women quickly exited the stage, and just as the applause was dying down, the male dancers took their place, lining up with arms linked. The music started out much the same way, slow and deliberate at first, gradually increasing in intensity and tempo until the excitement was at a peak. At this point, one man at the head of the line began to jump, contort, and fling himself into the air in a series of acrobatic moves that were astounding. Just as I thought, *How long can he keep this up?* he moved to the end of the line, allowing the next dancer to perform his own style of boot-slapping, heel-kicking, body-contorting dance moves. By the time the last man had his moment in the spotlight, I was exhausted for them. They took a simple bow and moved off stage towards their beers.

The musicians took a breath and continued on with the next song. Most of the music was played at a very loud volume (probably to be heard above the volume of Greek conversations in the audience), but nonetheless we enjoyed the experience, which was even more memorable because we were the only non-Greeks in the large crowd of almost 300.

As dusk crept up from the valleys to the hillsides, we made our way back to the car laughing and reminiscing about the day's events, grateful for yet another charmingly chaotic Greek venture to remember with each other. We fell into an exhausted silence as we wound our way down the curvy little road from the hills to home, skirting through acres and acres of trees profuse with the fruit of the gods and the promise of a good year's olive harvest.

OH, OLIVES!

THE MAGICAL FRUIT OF THE ISLAND

It's olive harvesting season on Crete, and the everyday sounds of autumn are intensified by the slapping, whirring sounds of the olive picking rods in nearby groves. If you were raised in a culture where this is an annual occurrence and, in fact, your livelihood depends on it, it is the sound of high hopes and hard work. But to these very American ears, it held all the attraction of quintessential Greece and an invitation to observe the ancient occupation of olive harvesting. I even entertained the idea of joining the workers in neighboring groves to immerse myself in the experience. But I soon discovered it was significantly less glamorous and notably more work than I expected.

S etting out on my bicycle one November afternoon, I took the dusty road down towards the sea and came upon a small group of neighbors hard at work under the shade of the short, stocky olive trees that were dripping with their magical green fruit. It appeared as though it was a family or families (two women, two men, and a young child) all suited up for a long day's work. Each had their own tasks, and they toiled together like a well-oiled machine. The men swiped at the tallest branches with the rotating rod that sent the olives flying off their perch and onto the mesh blankets that the women had carefully tucked around the tree trunks and spread out beyond their shade. It was dusty, sweaty, muscle-wrenching, finger-numbing work.

Occasionally, they gathered around a table and poured the hard green fruit into a box where the stems and leaves would be separated from the olives. Hardly the ideal machine, since much of the tedious work was still left to human hands to trim the olives that had somehow escaped the machinery. Nevertheless, they were in good spirits and chatted and laughed as they nimbly worked their fingers through the olives and foliage.

Their good-natured smiles emboldened me to venture into their world for a moment and ask if I could observe and take a few photos. I told them in my broken Greek that I lived just up the hill and was on a bike ride around the neighborhood. The women warmly welcomed me into the grove of blue-green trees, and in rapid fire Greek, with the aid of exaggerated hand motions, they educated me in the art of the olive harvest. These trees were obviously a source of the pride and promise of another year of good oil. We shared in a few laughs, and it wasn't until I caught a glimpse of mild annoyance from one of the men that I realized it was time to exit so they could get back to work. They graciously posed for some photographs, and in the typical Greek way, didn't let me leave empty-handed. I stuffed the handful of olives and twigs into my backpack, waved a cheerful goodbye, and thanked them for including me in a small but important part of their existence.

The process of gathering olives is tremendously hard work that involves everyone in the family as well as many immigrant workers from Bulgaria and northern parts of Greece. The olive trees are dripping with the "fruit of the gods," and there is something about these olives that bring out a sense of Cretan national pride. After all, the best olive oil in the world is claimed to come from Crete and certainly the Cretans have had plenty of centuries to perfect the craft. Even the ancient Minoans (3000 BC) appreciated the olive for its divine properties.

The reward for the hard labor of olive harvesting is iridescent, green, extra virgin, cold-pressed, organic olive oil that explodes with peppery taste and makes anything you put it on or in taste like comfort food. A trip to an olive oil factory is a lesson in Greek culture. The Cretan factories range from primitive but efficient in the small villages to the shiny sophisticated operations in the larger cities. We visited a factory outside of Hania on the National Highway on one November morning. It was buzzing with activity and humming with the sound of machinery as the olives traveled through their progression from the large burlap bags to the final press. They were shaken, de-stemmed, pitted, washed, pressed, stirred, and liquified. Everything was used. The stems and leaves were sucked up into a large pipe that extended out to the yard where a pile as tall as the building waited for farmers to come by and shovel the greenery into their little trucks to be used as feed for goats and sheep. Likewise, the pits were launched into a waiting dump truck that would transport the load to other factories where they would be pressed again and used for olive oil products like soaps and lotions, as well as cheaper oil. In most cases, there is an arrangement of payment for both the factory and the hard-working harvesters by giving them a percentage of the final product of extra virgin oil.

A little-known fact is that the average Greek consumes 20 liters of olive oil per year. That means an average family of four consumes 80 liters (or over 20 gallons) per year. When I confirmed that astounding fact to my Greek friends, they just shrugged and said, "That's about right." But then, olive oil in Crete is as plentiful as water. In fact, every authentic Greek recipe and remedy involves the use of copious amounts of olive oil. Need a skin lotion or sunscreen? Rub in a little olive oil. Want to lubricate a creaky door hinge? A few drops of olive oil will do the trick. Hair mask? Olive oil. Dry lips? Olive oil. Bee sting, rash, or mosquito bite? You get the point. Some remedies really should get a prize for the most creative. A Greek friend swears that a precautionary couple of teaspoonfuls of olive oil before a night out on the town will ease the effects of alcohol (presumably so you can drink even more) and that the same treatment after a drinking binge will ease the effects of a morning hangover.

I thought I'd heard it all until I was the unfortunate recipient of yet another fender-bender in my already scarred Honda. An older Greek gentleman didn't acknowledge (or didn't see) a stop sign and his front bumper met the side of my car in a slow-motion metal-on-metal grind as I passed through the intersection. Luckily, there was no dent, but there was a huge scratch the length of my car where his bumper had met my driver's side. The narrow street in downtown Hania was crowded with passing pedestrians, and as he and I waited for the local police to arrive, we were the focus of curiosity. More than once, an older woman stopped to inspect the large scratch on my car and offer her sage advice. It was always the same. *Tipota! Ligo lathi!* Which, roughly translated means, "It's nothing! Put a little olive oil on it!" To which I could only respond, "Seriously? Even if it worked, why would I want to waste this liquid gold on my *car*?"

I put on a few pounds after we moved to the island, mostly due to the abundance of feta and bread. There's nothing really special about the bread; it just serves as a conduit to get the olive oil into my mouth without using a straw. I often wondered how it would look to stash away a purse-sized flask of olive oil and a lemon when we traveled off the island. It really is that good. And I've learned to be very generous with the oil in all my recipes. I may not have hit the 20 liters per year number but I bet I'm close.

Aside from the constant activity of the olive or grape harvests, autumn on Crete provides the perfect ambiance to explore many other diversions to occupy mind and body. The mild temperatures are perfect for the road trips, bike trips, and hiking trips that were put on hold while the summer heat keeps most of humanity near the beaches. We indulged in all three, ticking the items off our must-see list that grew longer as more time went by.

FROM SEA TO SHINING SEA
A SLICE OF CRETE ROAD TRIP

The longer we're here the more attached we have become to this unusual island that hums with the hybrid intensity of modern-day tourism and ancient traditions.

Every day on Crete was an opportunity to discover the good and the bad, the ugly and the magnificent, wrapped up in unfamiliar packaging. I often satisfied my creative itch to write or photograph simply by walking on the beach in any season, in any weather. The ever-changing sea and sky was inspiration enough to fill my mind with ideas and my heart with gratitude. But, leaving the beach behind me to venture up into the hills of Crete was an opportunity to discover the "real Crete."

One autumn weekend Richard and I packed up the car and headed southeast, over the neck of Crete and down to the south coast. At its skinniest point, Crete is only about thirty-five miles wide with a spine of mountains (Lefka Ori or White Mountain range in the west and Psiloritis range towards the east) running down the center of the island dividing the north coast from the south. Skirting along the water's edge on the national highway reminded me a little of driving Highway 1 in California. The highway hugged the coastline, weaving around rocky coves and bridging deep gorges. But that is where the similarity stopped. Driving this stretch of highway was nothing like driving in California.

The national highway that spans east to west across the northern shore of Crete has its own set of unspoken rules. The road is a wide, two-lane highway with ample shoulders. We soon discovered that the "correct" way to drive this road is to use the shoulder frequently to yield to faster moving vehicles. Other cars approaching in the opposite direction know this "rule" as well and they take to the shoulder, too. The result is a strange weaving motion between the main lanes and the shoulders. The straight highway is rarely driven straight. But once you get used to this crazy way of driving and abide by the unwritten rules of the road, it actually flows pretty well. We learned quickly not to panic at the sight of an oncoming vehicle in our lane.

After years of driving on the roads of Crete, we tolerated and even joined in on this crazy dance, calmly moving into the shoulder in order to keep the flow going. Surprising and refreshing is the lack of road rage. Most drivers on Crete definitely have a crazy style, but one thing you can count on is that they won't lift their fist (or finger) at you on the road.

We let out a sigh of relief when we finally exited the national highway at Vrisses and headed south on the familiar two-lane road that snaked up into the hills and towards the south coast. Immediately, the scenery changed and soon we were well entrenched in the wild and harsh *Sfakia* territory. This area has a reputation for authentic Cretan traditions as well as being home to some of the proudest and fiercest freedom fighters in its long history of foreign occupation (case in point: the proud artistry of the Cretan Sfakian knife.) Sfakia has been described as wild, dangerous, backwoods, stubborn, proud, simple and mysterious. A deep intrigue seeps out of the untamed beauty of the rugged landscape and the modest, timeworn villages. As the road passes through mountain villages with names like Vamos and Embrosneros, it becomes very clear that Sfakia is refreshingly unstained from the rampant tourism of the coastal areas.

The road took us through the fertile Askifou Plateau, over the high hills, through tunnels skirting the spectacular Imbros Gorge, and back out to the sea on the south side. As we wound our way down the high hills, we rounded a corner and suddenly the Libyan Sea spread out before us like a blanket of glittering silk. The horizon melted into the hot sky where it disappeared over the edge of the world. The road perched high above the coast and dropped dramatically in a series of hairpin turns backed with breathtaking views. At sea level, we turned east and stopped in at the site of *Frangokastello*, an old castle fortress built originally in 1371 and inhabited by the Venetians, then the Turks, then finally a Cretan revolutionary named Daliani in 1828. He and his small force of rebels were martyred there during the Turkish occupation and have become heroic legends that, according to locals, appear as ghosts in the morning mist around dawn every year on May 17th.

No area of Crete is left untouched by the destruction and

abuses of occupying foreign forces over the centuries. But this particular day was quiet, clear, and serene, so we stopped and jumped in the ocean for a refreshing swim before continuing on to the seaside town of Plakia. A thriving tourist town in the summer, Plakia was just now breathing the first of its off-season sighs, and the autumn pulse in the air was calm and cheerful. We went to a local taverna to inquire about a room in their small and rustic family run hotel, Gioma. Our room overlooked the sea and the balcony was draped with a huge magenta-colored bougainvillea vine—all for €35.

Later that evening, we sat at a small table in a delightful fish taverna on the water. After selecting our fish from the daily catch on ice, we settled in over a glass of wine to enjoy the sunset. As the last light of day dissolved into the motionless sea, the lights from the harbor gently appeared, their glow reflecting off the water like slow-dancing fireflies.

The next day, we set out traveling east towards the Preveli Monastery (Moni Preveli) set high on a hill above the sea. On the way, we stopped in the little village of Rodakino (which means peach) to buy some local honey before continuing on past the older ruins of the lower Preveli Monastery. We arrived at the upper monastery early in the afternoon—the hottest part of the day. The warm whisper of a breeze from the south provided very little comfort, but our energy was renewed as we approached the monastery and entered its gates.

As we walked the hushed corridors and courtyards of the monastery grounds, we felt as if we had stepped back in time. The grounds were impeccably cared for, and there was obviously a lot of thought put into attracting and educating visitors from Crete and beyond. Special exhibitions in the on-site museum detailed the current monastic lifestyle, as well as the rich history of Moni Preveli during various uprisings. Its mark in history was as a center for resistance during the Turkish occupation and then later during the World War II invasion of Crete by German troops.

This German invasion, called the Battle of Crete (Operation Mercury), was the most significant event in modern Cretan history. Although the battle technically lasted for only ten days, the losses were staggering on both sides. Because of its strategic position in the Mediterranean, Allied forces (primarily Brits and Aussies) held military strongholds to defend the island during the early days of the War. But on May 20th, the Germans launched an airborne invasion (the first in history) to occupy the island. The German invaders suffered unprecedented losses, a vast number of them being shot out of the sky as they parachuted down towards land. But over the next few days, they gained the upper hand and moved through western Crete, forcing the evacuation of many Allied troops.

Countless stories of bravery and resolve are recorded as hundreds of Allied soldiers painstakingly made their way through rocky, precipitous gorges towards the south coast. Many never made it—dying of hunger and exposure. But the ones that did were saved largely due to the fierce fighting of the Cretan resistance fighters and brave civilians that held off the German pursuit. This resolute and unexpected defiance infuriated the Germans, who resorted to brutal reprisals during the following years of occupation. Mass executions were common, as was arson and the complete annihilation of entire villages that had given refuge to many of the fleeing Allied soldiers.

The Preveli Monastery is a living monument from the Battle of Crete because it played a significant part in saving countless Allied lives. Perched high above the Libyan Sea, it is forever etched in history as a safe haven for British and Australian troops who fled there from the north coast through the Imbros Gorge in order to escape capture by the German troops. The Allied troops that survived the rugged and harsh mountain terrain were taken in, hidden, and cared for by the abbot Langouvardos, the residing monks, and the surrounding villagers in defiance of the German military and under threat of death. When the sick and wounded soldiers were strong enough, they were escorted under the cloak of darkness down the steep mountain path to the seashore where they were evacuated by submarine to safety in Egypt.

The nicely designed and very interesting museum is worth a visit, but the true beauty of Moni Preveli is found by just wandering around the grounds. An old fountain (circa 1701) graces the courtyard and bears an inscription that translates, "Clean my transgressions, not only my face." We sat in the shade of a giant eucalyptus tree in the courtyard shared by sleepy cats and gazed out over the Libyan Sea. The sounds of a bleating sheep and the soft ring of a goat bell competed with a raucous cry of a peacock in the monastery barnyard below. A peek into the small chapel in the middle of the monastery revealed much of the same ornate interior as most Greek Orthodox churches. The serene and dimly lit interior revealed painted frescoes of the saints, prayer icons, and the lingering scent of incense. Everything was so steeped in tradition and old-worldliness that it was quite a shock to the senses when a residing priest whipped out his iPhone from under his black robe and struck up a conversation with us about his favorite apps. We were still chuckling about that as we exited the monastery and drove north through the short but dramatic Kourtaliotiko Gorge.

As we traveled out of the gorge, a small nondescript wooden sign beckoned us to check out the Cretan Folk Museum in the village of Assomatos. This privately owned museum, located in an old Cretan stone house, contained historical implements of the past including traditional Cretan clothing, cooking accessories, books, Cretan knives, photos, and fiber art like handmade blankets and rugs. The place was packed with everything from the wondrous to the weird. We exited after a good hour of snooping around in the museum and remarked with some smugness at how smart we were to not hurry by.

If there's one thing we've learned in our travels, it's to resist the temptation to overplan and over schedule. It's easy to come up with a "must-see" travel list, and much harder but more gratifying to adopt the "we'll see" attitude of spontaneity. Of course, as counterintuitive as it may sound, the ability to enjoy spontaneity takes upfront strict planning. For example, if the road trip from point A to point B takes two hours to drive straight through, plan on three and keep your eyes open. You never know what gems you may discover.

Driving out of Assomatos towards the north coastal city of Rethymno, I pondered the meaning of something I had read earlier that morning. Jesus said in Matthew 6:34, *"Give your entire attention to what God is doing right now, and don't get worked up about what may or may not happen tomorrow. God will help you deal with whatever hard things come up when the time comes."* (The Message).

I wondered how much I had missed in my life because I was either fretting about the past or worrying about the future, and I realized that both have enormous power to steal *joy* from the here and now. In every fleeting moment there is a beauty to behold, but we tend to look for the miraculous in the obvious: a stunning mountaintop view, a night illuminated with a galaxy of stars, a vibrant sunset over the sea, a newborn baby. All these things take my breath away, it's true, and I will continue to marvel at God's enormous creativity. But let me not become so engrossed in looking ahead for the next exciting adventure or the next impressive photo that I miss the mystery of small miracles in this present moment: cool water on a hot day, the sunlight passing through tall branches, the soft song of a mother, and the very breath in my body that gives me the ability to whisper, "Thank you!"

HEROES AND HUMOR
THE STORY OF KAPSALIANA

L ife is the unpredictable mixture of tragedy and comedy; little and big events that bring out the heroic and the humorous. What started out as an anniversary getaway in November, ended up being a surprise visit back into the essence of old Crete. Kapsaliana Village, located up in the hills above Rethymno, was once a small but thriving settlement that existed purely for the purpose of pressing olives. Abbot Filaretos of the nearby Arkadi Monastery (established in 1600) built the olive mill in 1763 in order to provide the community with the precious sacred oil of the olives. At its height of prosperity, the settlement of Kapsaliana had roughly 50 people, all of whom worked at the mill. It flourished for over 200 years, until in the mid-1900s the monastery closed down the mill and moved it to another location. The population of Kapsaliana dwindled after the mill was closed and the deserted village eventually crumbled into ruin and became another Greek ghost town.

For over thirty years, the stones of the historic olive mill succumbed to weeds and would have surely decayed into obscurity had it not been for an architect from Heraklion, Crete with a love for historical heritage and a big vision. In 1980, Myron Toupoyannis purchased the entire site and began the painstaking restoration of converting the old ruins into one of Crete's most distinctive and idyllic retreats. The 300-year-old hamlet set amidst the vast olive groves of the Arkadi Monastery has been converted into comfortable guest bungalows, a main house with a restaurant, gardens, and a relaxing pool with a view of the sea. Every effort was made to preserve the historical integrity of the village and the original olive press and surrounding workshops present like a museum. All the modern comforts of a fastidiously decorated dwelling are balanced with the historic traditions of the period. And just like many other villages in Crete, the history of this area has its heart-wrenching stories.

The Arkadi Monastery played an active role in the heroic Cretan resistance of the Ottoman rule. During the Cretan revolt in 1866, a horrendous massacre by the Turks occurred at the monastery where 964 Greeks, mostly women and children, had sought refuge. On November 8th, the assault began with the Turks having the clear advantage—thousands of Turkish fighters with thirty cannons against less than 200 Cretan men armed only with rifles and knives. After three days of battle the last of the Cretan fighters fell and the 80-year-old abbot of the monastery gathered up the remaining people, mostly women and children, and hid in the powder keg room. When the Turks arrived at the door, the abbot set the barrels of gunpowder on fire, choosing to sacrifice themselves rather than surrender. Today, a visit to the still active monastery reveals peaceful gardens and golden hued stone walls. But the powder room has never been restored. The roof is gone, and the charred remains of the walls stand as a memorial to those who lost their lives there 150 years ago.

During the days that we stayed at Kapsaliana Village we took advantage of the good weather to hike and bike around the hills. On Sunday, we rode our bikes a few miles down the narrow country road and stumbled upon a tiny little pedestrian-only village nestled down in a creek-side ravine. At first blush, Pirkis seemed to be a nondescript typical Cretan village that even the guidebooks missed. But we discovered remnants of Venetian influence in the architecture indicating this town had been around for quite a while—over 500 years to be exact. The biggest surprise was an old treasure tucked back into one of its alleys in an obscure, forgotten spot. Behind a group of old stone homes was the ancient Venetian gate to the city, a stone arch with a mantle that bore a faded Latin inscription, *Pateat Bonis*, meaning "be open to good."

As we peddled through this village lost in time, we were keenly aware of blatant stares from the locals. The sight of two Americans on bicycles in a remote village just doesn't happen every day. But the villagers were engaging, speaking rapid Greek to us and laughing at their jokes like we could understand every word. As we were waiting for the bread man to deliver the morning's goods, I asked two older women if I could take their photo. The elder of the women was very shy, but her friend grabbed her and made her chuckle. Of all the photos I take in my travels, my favorites are of sweet smiles like the ones I captured on these women in the village of Pirkis.

On our way back to Hania and home, we stopped at a stable in Georgioupolis, where I had arranged for a horseback ride on the beach. Our guide was an enormous Greek fellow who straddled the back of his horse with amazing agility and grace. He led us down the path towards the sea and we walked casually along the shoreline for about a kilometer. The conversation between the three of us was centered on horses, family, and the Cretan beauty around us.

Soon, he turned to us and asked with a twinkle in his eye, "Do you want to run?" I hardly had time to say yes when he and Richard took off at a full gallop, leaving me behind. As I urged my little mare to catch up with the boys, she pulled out the stops and sprinted after them. We finally caught up with the other two, only to be covered by the wet sand they were kicking up in their frantic wake. My little mare turned out to be a hellion, as she was clearly enjoying the romp while I was trying desperately to see out of my sand-caked sunglasses. All previous visions of a romantic ride on the beach with my golden tan and my hair flowing behind me were destroyed. When we finally stopped after an exhilarating run, I was covered from head to foot with wet, sticky sand. The looks on the faces of our guide and my husband said it all. I was an incredible mess and we all had a good laugh at my expense. All the way back to the stables and in the car trip home, I was digging sand out of my ears, nostrils, and teeth.

Back home, Richard unpacked the car from our memorable road trip to Kapsaliana. He cleaned up our bikes, unloaded our suitcases and cooler, fed the dog, opened the windows, and made dinner. I took a long, hot shower, thankful that the physical abuse on my body was over. Or I thought it was.

Only a few weeks later, my avid cycling husband got it into his mind to take on the challenge of riding the road from seaside up into the White Mountains of Crete. While HIS passion is enjoying the trek on the saddle of a bicycle, I much prefer different modes of transportation that allow me to photograph and eat through the journey. However, somehow I got talked into riding this one with him.

At first I declined, but when I found out that a friend was going to drive the sag wagon for us, I figured I could always opt out if it got too tough and then default to the above-mentioned eating and photographing while the other crazed wheelies finished this insane quest. And I figured I'm not too proud to accept help, mostly because I don't have a competitive bone in my body.

I was wrong.

BIKE TREKS AND A STACK OF WAFFLES
SCREAMING LEGS AND KILLER VIEWS

*OK Road Warriors, THE RIDE is upon us! Tomorrow. 0800.
Starbucks. Hania port. Leave at 0830 after a jolt of espresso.
Weather looks to be STELLAR! 20C (68F) at sea level. When
we leave the port, it should be about 16C/60F, however we are
climbing. We are ascending almost 5,000 feet, so assume the high
temp at the top will be no more than 12C/50F. Bring water, air
tubes/patches, and light snacks. Layer for changing weather as well.
Check your bike out before the big day. . . brakes, gears, and air in
your tires. Need I say more? Get a good night's sleep.*

Rider of the Cretan Mountains,
— Richard (email to fellow bikers)

We started out the morning at Starbucks in the old Hania
port area, tanking up on a good jolt of espresso before
heading out on our road bikes. The original team of four core
bikers dropped to three when one got stuck in Athens due to
(another) ferry strike. The morning was clear and cool. A perfect

start. Our dedicated sag wagon driver and her friend joined us at Starbucks, and after a few small adjustments to bikes, comparing notes on apparel, and synchronizing our trip plans, we peddled out through the streets of Hania, heading southwest towards the mountains. Spirits were high, as only veteran bikers understand when you head out on a long, arduous ride. With the thrill of the goal ahead of us, all logic dissipated and we were off, with smiles on our faces and high hopes under our helmets.

Destination: Just past the Omalos plateau to Xyloskalo where most hikers begin their trek of the Samaria Gorge as it cuts deeply and dramatically into the mountains.
Distance: 43.3 km of switchbacks and ridiculous ascents.
Altitude: From sea level to 1,400 meters (4,600 feet)
Time: Anywhere from 3 hours to . . . tomorrow.

Heading out from the port was an easy warm-up grade for about 16 km (10 miles) after which we hit nine switchbacks ascending to the beautiful mountain village of Lakki in the foothills of the Lefka Ori (White Mountain) range. We arrived in Lakki in good shape ready for a breather before tackling the meat of the ride. Feeling strong and overly optimistic, I had no idea what was a head of me. What you don't know, won't hurt you—that is, until it does.....painfully.

Peddling out of Lakki, it wasn't long before our third rider ("the young buck") motored ahead of us, leaving us in his dust. We didn't see him again until the top. My devoted husband rode with me for a few miles before I unselfishly released him and he happily engaged his "motor legs" to sprint on ahead. I only saw the back of him for a few minutes before he peddled out of sight. A strange feeling of calm peppered with a slight touch of anxiety came over me as I realized my "aloneness" in this vast mountain moonscape. But the freedom I felt as I settled into my own pace and allowed myself to totally engage in the experience was strangely stimulating. As I propelled up the hills and around multiple switchbacks, I found a rhythm that worked for me, so that even when our sag wagon pulled up next to me and offered rest and a ride, I declined.

The landscape after Lakki is an entirely different animal. In fact, the road, although still paved, is mostly frequented not by cars and people, but by herds of goats and sheep sunbathing on the warm patches of asphalt.

> *The landscape after Lakki is no longer "human." There are no orange groves and no cultivated lands, nothing to remind one of how man "tames" nature. The road climbs suddenly through steep mountain slopes with tall cedar trees and thick bushes, and as it climbs it offers a spectacular view. Be careful, though, because it has many dangerous hairpins. About 15 km south of Lakki, at a height of 1200 m, the road goes through a pass from which you have a sudden view of Omalos Plateau some 200 meters lower. From early fall until the end of spring, the mountain peaks surrounding the plateau are covered with snow. In the spring the snow melts and the plateau is turned into a huge swamp or even a lake. Those*

parts that are not covered by water are full of wildflowers. (Alpha-Omega Travel)

From Lakki to the Samaria Gorge trailhead, the road was far steeper than anticipated and required focus and a good dose of pride to keep on going. Did I mention insanity? But the anticipation of reaching the goal was motivation enough to keep cranking. When I finally crested the pass, my spirits (and bike) soared as I flew down the short but sweet descent into the high plateau of Omalos. The end was in sight—at least psychologically. I still had what turned out to be the hardest part of the ride ahead of me: two kilometers of straight but steady incline to the end point at the top of the Samaria Gorge.

By now, the false summit had faked me out and I was physically and emotionally exhausted, but somewhere deep down, I willed myself to continue on.

Competitiveness? Long gone.

A story to tell? Forget it.

Just the idea that I hadn't come this far to quit now was the single thing that kept me going; That, and a good dose of cheerleading from my husband who rode down to join me for the last kilometer.

Turns out I wasn't too far behind after all, coming in to the finish line a mere 15 minutes after him. After climbing for over three hours to an altitude of 1400 m (4,600 feet), I was rewarded with stellar views over the Samaria Gorge, a cold glass of Mythos beer, mouth-watering *souvlaki* (Greek fast food) at an Omalos taverna, and crowing rights with good friends as insane as me.

I say insane, because that's the only way I can explain why we tackled it again the following spring, taking a longer but gentler route coming in the back way and ending at the Omalos Plateau. Maybe it was that big stack of pre-ride killer Belgian waffles that made me feel so brave.

> *"What better way to carb-load before an epic ride than to tank up on a break-feast of Richard's Belgium waffles smothered with homemade peanut butter and pure maple syrup, steaming sausages, fresh-squeezed orange juice and rich, black espresso.*
> *Ready to ride!"*

As spring approached, we set our sights again on conquering the heights of the road to Omalos. As we had discovered the previous fall, this epic ride was not for the faint of heart or the ill-prepared, so we set off to stretch and strengthen our bike legs on a couple of weekend excursions around our own Akrotiri peninsula. Riding around the Akrotiri that spring was one way to get our bike legs in shape before conquering the BIG ONE . . . again.

> *Saturday morning, March 17, sunny but cool St. Patrick's Day. The "luck of the Irish" (and the good Lord) was with these riders—five guys and a lady (someone had to keep all that testosterone in check.) We were a ragtag bunch of roadies composed of a British newbie, a couple of Greek iron men, two 50+ American youngsters, and an Italian stud on a knobby-tired mountain bike.*

Rather than take the typical route to Omalos like we did on our ride in October, we took the road less traveled starting just outside Alikianos. We headed west towards Sougia, a longer but more scenic and presumably gentler climb. Almost immediately, the two iron men sprinted ahead, leaving the rest of us to pace ourselves and enjoy the companionship of the ride. Along the way, we experienced the expected (a flat tire) and the unexpected (an attack of angry bees), but nothing could compare with the new rush of adrenaline that we shared when we crested the ridge where the wind turbines stood.

We had heard their eerie call many kilometers downhill before we arrived in their massive shadow. Their slow, rhythmic "whoop, whoop, whoop" was strangely calming in the midst of heart-pounding physical exertion. We stopped under their massive blades at the top of the mountain road to catch our breath and take in the extraordinary panorama. The view over our left shoulder was north over the Aegean and over our right shoulder was south over the Libyan Sea.

We were perched on the backbone of Crete.

A vista of huge proportions took what was left of our breath away. And because there was something so satisfying about riding to the top of the ridge on bikes instead of in a car, we felt extra deserving of the amazing sight in front of us. But the ride wasn't over, and the last 12 km was the hardest.

As we headed behind the wind turbines and up the scenic gorge, our legs started screaming for the finish. Finally, after roughly thirty miles and four hours of hill climbing from just above sea level to 4,500 feet elevation, we were at the finish point where the pristine, snow-covered sleepy and expansive Omalos plateau stretched out before us.

I seriously doubt that Winston Churchill was a cyclist, but somehow he connected with cyclists everywhere when he said, "There will stretch out before you an ever-lengthening, ever-ascending, ever-improving [OK, that's debatable] path . . . But this, far from being discouraging, only adds to the joy and glory of the climb."

The road to the heights of the Samaria Gorge is definitely bikeable, albeit challenging, but descending down into the gorge is only for robust travelers on foot. Sitting at a table in the taverna, I looked down at the gaping jaws of the deep gorge. I marveled at the breathtaking view of the mountain peaks that soar up to almost 3000 meters while nibbling on a warm honey-drizzled *sfakia pie*. Sweet memory of Omalos. So sweet in fact, it was tempting to linger there, order up another pie with a hot cup of mountain tea and just be an armchair observer of the Samaria trekkers. But I knew I couldn't exit the island without hiking this famous big daddy of all gorges at least once.

HIKING THE BIG ONE
THE SAMARIA GORGE

One of the perks of being a full-time resident of a destination such as Crete, is the opportunity to wait out the tourist season and enjoy the sights at a more leisurely pace of our choosing. Such was the case when it came to my experience hiking the Samaria Gorge. A group of girlfriends and I decided to wait out the hot, crowded summer months and make the trek at the end of October before the gorge closed for the winter. The date was set, but when we woke up that morning to chilly, overcast skies and a slight drizzle, most of my friends dropped out until only two of us were left.

"So, what do you think?" I asked my trekking companion, Lisa.

I could hear a short pause of indecision on the other end of the phone but she replied, "I think we should give it a try. It might be our last chance before the gorge is closed for the winter."

"All right. I'm in. Let's do this!" We decided to go ahead with the plan, determined not to let the dreary weather dampen our resolve or our quest for crowing rights.

The Samaria Gorge, AKA *Farangas* (Great Gorge) is arguably the longest gorge in Europe and remains the most visited spot on Crete by hikers and nature lovers from all over the world. The National Park of Samaria is located just outside of the high plateau village of Omalos in the White Mountains of western Crete, 43 km from the port city of Hania. This untamed and impressive park draws busloads of visitors that come to hike the most popular trail on the island.

The Samaria Gorge is a spectacular canyon, a great gash in the mountains of Crete boasting stunning views and rich ecosystems (450 different plant species and home to the famous wild kri-kri goat indigenous to Crete). This hike is part of the extensive E-4 trail (European Mountaineering Footpath originating in Spain) that traverses the island west to east and crosses many mountain ranges including the Lefka Ori.

Because the Samaria Gorge is such a popular hiking destination, the crowds are relentless in the summer months. Up to 3,000 visitors a day snake down the long footpath following the creek bed that cuts through the gorge. In the summer months, it is a four to six hour sizzling hot, dry, rocky hike with an ever-moving stream of tourists, some well outfitted in good hiking shoes and others looking like they just came from the beach. Just a side note: if you want to hike the gorge successfully, leave the flip-flops at home.

The trailhead begins at *Xyloskalo*, meaning "wooden staircase" on the upper rim of the Omalos Plateau. Here the trail drops precipitously down into the gorge over a series of switchbacks that have replaced the original makeshift "staircase" originally used by the locals for access into the gorge.

Because of weather, the gorge is open roughly from mid-April to the end of October. The winter rains and snowmelt transform the creek's summer trickle to a dangerous roaring river that rushes through the narrow canyon moving shrubs, trees, and even rocks out of its path before emptying itself and all its debris into the Libyan Sea.

The usual way of hiking the gorge is by descending it from the top near the high plateau of Omalos (altitude 1,250 meters) and trekking the 18 km down to where the gorge spills out onto the shores of the sea. The small seaside fishing village of Agia Romeli sits nestled under a grove of tamarisk trees at the mouth of the gorge. Here is where most exhausted hikers conclude their trek after obsessing over the thought of the last few kilometers, *What do I do first when I reach Agia Romeli? Drown my thirst in a tall cold beer at the first taverna I see, or dive straight into the cool waters of the Med?* Some opt for both, nursing their beer as they sit in the water at the edge of the beach.

Because of weather and time constraints, Lisa and I decided to do the hike the opposite direction, beginning in Agia Romeli and hiking *up* the gorge. We boarded the first morning ferry at Hora Sfakia and chugged along the south coast through the fog to Agia Romeli, which is only accessible by foot or boat.

Forty-five minutes later, with no reprieve in the weather in sight, we arrived at Agia Romeli. Walking up to the entrance of the gorge past tavernas, mini markets, and tourist shops, it was hard to imagine that just a couple of months ago, they were busting at the seams with visitors.

On this particular day in late October, the village was closing up for the winter months. One tired -looking taverna was open; its only occupant the Greek owner scrubbing the summer dust and grime off the little wooden chairs and stacking them on top of the bright blue and green tables. After a smile and a quick greeting, we continued on behind the village to the gorge entrance gate where we purchased a ticket for a nominal price of €2 that we needed in order to exit the gorge (this policy is mainly for safety reasons to regulate the whereabouts of visitors in the gorge.)

The path became more interesting as it continued up the riverbed, which at this time of year, had diminished to a gentle trickle. A short distance ahead was the most photographed spot in the gorge, the *Portes* (doors) or as the locals call it, *Sideroportes* (Iron Gates).

"Wow! Check this out!"

Lisa was standing in the narrowest part of the gorge where the sheer rock walls, only three meters apart at their base, towered above her to an apex of over 300 meters. I took a photograph of her outstretched arms, but her size diminished to a speck on my lens in comparison to the colossal cliffs. Continuing further into the gorge, we passed under vertical walls of rock and stopped occasionally to rest and drink cold, clear spring water from the stone-built fountains that were strategically placed along the path.

Around every corner a new magnificent rock formation loomed over us, shading a wild array of Cretan flora: the cypress and pine trees, as well as seasonal wildflowers, and the scarce dittany herb known for its medicinal benefits. The famous kri-kri goats eluded us, but there were many birds, and best of all, very few people. Since we were not trying to break any records, we ambled along, enjoying the scenery and stopping frequently for photographs. The steady drizzle of moisture was the constant companion to our silent footsteps.

As we arrived at the deserted village of Samaria, the rain began to increase from a drizzle to a steady downpour. With thoughts of flash-flood warnings running through our heads, we made the decision not to go any further and turned around to make the trek back across slippery rocks, down muddy paths and an over an ever-increasing swath of river. We arrived back in Agia Romeli just in time to take in some refreshment at a taverna and catch the last ferry back to our car at Hora Sfakia.

During the long drive back over the mountains to the north coast and home, I silently reflected on the dramatic environment that had seen little change since the first civilizations that inhabited this isolated area of Crete. The creek path we trod in the gorge had been used centuries before, not for recreational hiking but for hunting and gathering, a highway to the sea from the upper heights for animals and ancient people alike. Cretans from ages past had gazed on the same walls of the soaring cliffs that we had marveled at today. I smiled as I thought to myself, *Who needs a time machine when you've got Crete?*

The night settled in, and so did a dense fog as we inched our way over the mountains and back down to the other side of the island towards home. I turned on the heat in the car for the first time since early last Spring. Our mild October weather was a mere memory now. Winter was quickly descending on the island.

WINTER

"Even beasts of burden must be turned out to grass occasionally;
the very sea pauses at ebb and flood; earth keeps the Sabbath of the
wintry months; and man, even when exalted to God's ambassador,
must rest or faint, must trim his lamp or let it burn low; must
recruit his vigor or grow prematurely old . . . in the long run we
shall do more by sometimes doing less."

— Charles Spurgeon

Winter on Crete brings a drastic halt to the frenetic energy of tourist summer and harvest autumn. The sleepy silence of an island at rest descends upon the land, interrupted only by the occasional tempest of miserable weather. The horizontal rain, blasting winds, and chilling temps can be depressing. But worst of all is the strange phenomenon of dirty "fog" that blows in from the northern deserts of Africa (dubbed *Khadafi dust)* clogging the air with thick red powder that settles on every surface and in every crack.

Other than the weather, winter life on the island is normally very quiet . . . extremely quiet . . . yawn . . . Zzzzzz. Most restaurants, shops, and sites are closed, and the locals take advantage of this sleepy time of year to relax, refresh, and rejuvenate. Spring will come soon enough, and with it, the drive to repaint, repair, and restore winter's damage. The weather provides the necessary R&R (rest and rain) to prepare for the hot, dry, busy months of summer.

It's tempting to spend the winter months indoors eating, drinking, and resting up for the excitement of the coming spring and summer. But the cooler temperatures and frequent clear days are perfect for that long hike or bike ride with the path ahead virtually empty of people. With the cooler temps and fewer visitors, the island breathes with a different rhythm and a more interesting medley of colors, sounds and scents.

We are reminded each day to slow down and keep our eyes wide open to the "God Sightings" all around us including the magnificent snow covered Lefka Ori mountain range that shadows Hania and the Aegean Sea in western Crete. We've learned we can live very comfortably with a fraction of our belongings, and that life doesn't revolve around our e-devices and overcommitted agendas. There's always time for a long walk or a long lunch (even if it's Greek style – 3 hours) and a smile and an easy "hello" is the universally understood sign of kindness no matter where in the world you are. Maybe it's the water – it just seems second nature to slow down, ease in and immerse yourself in the moment.

Each season brings its distinct beauty and purpose. This is the season of lazy fireside lunches in stone tavernas; the season of wine tastings at local wineries. This is the season of long, slow dinners with family and friends, and the season of storytelling.

THE GREEK STORYTELLER

"Stories have to be told or they die, and when they die, we can't remember who we are or why we're here."

—Sue Monk Kidd

"**M**y great–grandparents, Konstantinos and Ekaterina, eloped from Crete when they were just teenagers and boarded a small boat bound for Turkey. Turkey had a large population of immigrant Greeks back then. The trip across the sea took many days and was treacherous. They were fearful for their future, but of course, they were in love." Nick chuckled and winked at his wife, Marina. "Love is blind, you know,"

We were sharing a long, relaxing meal with a local couple from Hania, Nick and Marina, whom we met on the island almost immediately after moving there. Nick came from a long line of Cretan characters with intriguing stories. He had that uncanny ability to draw you in and make you believe the story he was telling has never been told, even if you'd heard it before. And each time it only got better. But what made it so enjoyable was not so much the content of the story (although it was usually very colorful, funny, and heartwarming) but rather the delivery of the facts and feelings so eloquently pieced together.

Because Crete has a long history, until just recently, of occupation by various dictatorships that hoped to crush its spirit, almost every family has well-protected tales of family history passed down through the generations. Rudyard Kipling once wrote, "If history were taught in the form of stories, it would never be forgotten." This observation couldn't be truer in the case of Greek culture.

With bellies full of satisfying Cretan cuisine and the wine still pouring, I knew it was the perfect time to ask Nick for a story or two—specifically a little recollection passed on through the generations about the "old days." He was more than happy to oblige.

He continued his story, "My great-grandparents started their new life in Constantinople, modern-day Istanbul, and raised their two sons there. They never returned to Crete."

But peace was fleeting, and in 1919, a turbulent period of intense Greek persecution began with the outbreak of the Greco-Turkish war in Turkey. Nick's face became serious when he shared the story of one of the sons who would be his grandfather.

"In the early 1900s, the Turks started forcing young Greek men to serve in their army. Nikolaos, my grandfather, was one of them. Turkish authorities gathered up dozens of young men in Nikolaos' neighborhood and marched them down the street away from their homes. The line of unwilling recruits grew longer as they marched on. At just the right moment Nikolaos saw an opportunity for escape and he took it. When the guards weren't looking, he ducked into a darkened doorway and hid, listening to the marching footsteps fade and disappear. The doorway led into a hospital, and the nurses who found him took pity on him and hid him in the basement. For six months, he lived in a tiny room that contained only a coal furnace."

One nurse in particular regularly served him food and water, and over time a friendship blossomed.

"By the time it was safe for him to come out of hiding, they were in love. She eventually became my grandmother, Maria."

Nick is most proud of the next part of the story and was more than happy to tell the details of his grandfather Nikolaos, whom he is named after.

"Nikolaos, was an accomplished singer, a very talented musician. After the war in Turkey, he studied Byzantine music at the university in Constantinople. He was still a student when the theological school at the Agia Triada monastery on Crete sent a request to his university for an instructor to serve at their school of Byzantine Music. It was a huge honor," Nick said proudly. "He took his wife and family and immigrated back to his roots on Crete. They went across the same stretch of water that his father and mother had sailed so many years ago."

Our conversation turned to more recent history, specifically World War II.

May 1941: Crete was under occupation yet again, this time by the Germans following the Battle of Crete. Prior to World War II, the Allies (primarily Brits and Australians) had established a defensive military presence on the island as friendly forces capitalizing on Crete's strategic location in the Med. Hitler's invasion of Crete changed the face of the island once again as his forces set out to capture or kill all Allies and anyone who got in the way of that campaign.

Nick described the bravery of the Cretan fighters, "Many Cretans fought alongside Allied troops and were responsible for saving Allied lives at the risk of their own lives and those of their loved ones and neighbors."

Historically, the Cretans are fiercely independent people and more than ready to join in the fight against any intruders. Most families can trace a relative or two who were immersed one way or another in resisting occupying forces. From the "freedom fighters" engaging in active combat to the quiet antagonists who did their part behind the scenes, the majority of families were not insulated from the difficulties and horrors of occupation and war.

"My mother and father lived in the city of Hania in northwest Crete, not far from the British airfield at Maleme, the first target of the German airstrike. You have to understand that although the Battle of Crete lasted only twenty days, mostly on the northern shores of Crete, the Cretan resistance movement was all over the island. They hated the German occupation, and whole villages risked everything to help the Allied forces fight back. My own family took part in the resistance against the Germans. My father worked for the Allies and the resistance fighters as a radio scrambler."

He explained that after the Germans established their dominion over most of Crete, martial law ensued and the possession of radios and firearms was strictly forbidden.

"My father kept his scrambler radio hidden under a floorboard of his bedroom, and when my mother swept the house, he would very carefully sprinkle a trace of dust over the board. One day a couple of German soldiers came to the house. You see, the Germans had suspected that there was a radio in the neighborhood and began a house-to-house search. My father had the radio carefully tucked away in its hiding place, but he still feared for his family if it were found. So you can imagine how he felt when one of the German officers went into the small, cramped bedroom. The officer stood directly on the movable floorboard but suspected nothing. Instead, he walked over to the bed where my father had hidden another piece of contraband under the mattress."

I realized we were holding our breath as Nick continued with the story.

"The cramped bedroom was very small. I mean, there was barely enough room to turn around in. The officer lifted one side of the mattress, and then went around and lifted the other side. Thank God for old Cretan beds! He never did find the German luger (gun) stashed right in the middle of the sagging mattress."

History tells us that many Cretans offered safe shelter for British soldiers at the risk of their own lives. Nick's family was no different. One day, long after the war, his aunt opened the front door to her small home in Hania to discover a tall British stranger and his wife on her doorstep.

Marina continued the story, "Nick's maternal grandfather Giorgos married Katerina and together they settled in a home in Hania. Beneath the house was a full basement with outbuildings, a wood shed, and a stable. During the occupation, a German official used the main house as his headquarters, and the family, including four children, was moved to the basement to live. They were expected to serve the Germans by running errands, cooking meals, and tending the garden. One of the daughters (Nick's mother, Marika) was an accomplished athlete and she ran messages for the British spies."

Nick continued the story, "My family hid a young British soldier by disguising him as a monk. They explained to the German officer that the reason he didn't respond to questions was because he was mute. Katerina and the children never told their father of the soldier in hiding. They were afraid that Giorgos would be killed along with the rest of the family if he were interrogated. Six months later, they managed to smuggle the Allied soldier named Jim through the Samaria Gorge with the aid of the Greek Resistance. He was evacuated by waiting Allied ships off the coast of Sfakia."

Marina smiled and added, "But the best part of the story is that thirty years later Jim returned to Crete to search for the family that saved his life. He went from door to door in our neighborhood of Nea Chora in Hania, knocking asking if anyone knew of a woman named Katerina with four children who lived in the neighborhood in the 1940s. With the help of neighbors, he found the house. Nick's aunt answered the door. He had returned to express his deep gratitude to the family that saved his life."

After a tearful reunion, he and his wife invited Nick's family to visit England. It took ten years, but eventually his aunt and her brother flew there to meet the rest of Jim's family. Among the many memories that they brought back to Crete with them, the most talked about was the copious amounts of tea they were offered during their visit by the "mute monk" and his English friends. Nick mimicked his aunt's incredulous question, "How much tea must people drink?"

Nick leaned back in his chair and laughed with his wife at the memory. He raised his glass in salute to the past, and we knew the storytelling had come to a close. We raised our glasses to his, and together we toasted the timeless blessings of family, freedom, and friends, without whom our stories would be no more than silent memories. I was keenly aware of the strong Greek value of family, and the tug of my own loved ones across the ocean pulled at my heart.

My heart was full of gratitude for Nick and Marina, our "family away from family." The crushing homesickness that would soon visit us was tolerable because of their friendship and the times spent with them were salve to our lonely souls. Stepping and sliding through the emotional ups and downs of living abroad brought me to my knees many times—sometimes in gratitude and sometimes in desperation. And more than once, I whispered the silent prayer of a lonely heart in winter's discontent.

THE WINTER BLUES
HOMESICKNESS SETS IN

This morning was quiet and overcast. A flat, colorless world pressed in from every window and made the house seem small and oppressive. A massive storm brewed in the north over the Aegean Sea, obscuring the horizon with a heavy gray mist. A pity party was in the making and the guest of honor was knocking at the door—depression. I was tempted to invite him in, but I knew he was the type of guest that always overstays his welcome. Instead, I threw my camera, my journal and a granola bar into my small backpack and walked out the door into the chilly air.

Autumn was full of the excitement of settling in to our new home, traipsing around the island every weekend and returning home to Colorado for a Christmas holiday visit. But then the winter months settled in on us, and so did our first taste of homesickness. While Richard ventured out every morning on his bicycle (rain or shine) to commute seven kilometers to his job on the Navy base, my autumn days of blissful outdoor activity diminished to primarily staying busy indoors while the wind howled and the rain slammed against the windowpanes. We weren't yet completely engaged as expats and were still getting our feet wet as Navy newbies. In other words, I wasn't home yet.

Some days, out of sheer desperation for human contact, I ventured on to the base and hung out at the library, the coffee shop or Graffiti's Diner where too many cheeseburger lunches eventually motivated me to sign up for fitness classes at the gym. A brutal but big-hearted British instructor, Sarah, whipped her minions into shape in no time, and I returned weekly only because the torture of her workouts was better than the torture of loneliness. Eventually meeting other American spouses with whom I had something in common was a Godsend. So was a spiritual community of people we met shortly after we arrived on the island.

Our first Sunday, we ventured down into the city to find a small church we had learned about on the internet. This small group of multi-cultural believers met in a basement room of the International Church of Hania. When we arrived we were greeted warmly and led into a low-ceilinged room packed with small straight-backed chairs and smiling people. When I heard at least three different languages of various European origins being spoken, it became very clear that this service would be a study in diversity.

The music began soon after we arrived. A woman from South Africa stepped up to the keyboard. Immediately, she launched into a rip-roaring, double-time version of an old hymn. Everyone was on their feet and sang in their own dialect with a vigor that matched her wide smile. Children wandered around the room, someone checked his cell phone, a woman lifted her hands in prayer and the space grew warm with energy. Someone turned on the little air-conditioning unit for which we were grateful, and I noticed the Greek and Bulgarian women pull their shawls closer around their necks.

Four songs later, a tall German gentleman stood and motioned for everyone to be seated. When he opened his mouth to speak I realized that he was the pastor, and he was going to preach the sermon...in German. The two men standing by his side were translators. The first translator decoded the words into Greek and/or Bulgarian before the second translator spoke it in English. A twenty-minute sermon took roughly forty minutes to translate...one sentence at a time. I noticed my 6'2" husband squirming uncomfortably in his undersized wooden chair and empathized with him as the pastor concluded his sermon, only to have a Bulgarian gentleman offer up a long prayer that was translated from Bulgarian to Greek to English.

An entire Sunday morning of this type of ping-pong linguistics was an auditory challenge; not to mention the time it took for a whole service to be translated. But there was something unearthly beautiful about so many different people all lifting up their voices in unity to sing or pray in their mother tongue to the Creator and Father of us all.

We usually left church spiritually satisfied but mentally exhausted and physically famished. It didn't take us long to adopt the routine of after-church taverna lunches with some of our best friends. Our first such outing was at the invitation of the South

African music leader and her family to join us at the beachside taverna in Kalathas on the Akrotiri. The owner, Tula (another South African transplant) was an extraordinary cook, and her open-air restaurant situated on the sands of Kalathas Beach was a local and tourist favorite that served up specialties like stuffed squash blossoms and oven-baked *gavdos* (sardines.) It was here at Tula's that we got our first glimpse of typical Greek restaurant protocol when it comes to kids.

Helene and Heinz had emigrated with their three children from South Africa to Crete a few years prior to our arrival and were solidly grounded on the island. So, it was no surprise that they had quickly adapted to the laidback, casual flow of island living. Here we were, two somewhat uptight Americans with our somewhat uptight manners, trying not to gawk and judge as their three kids gulped down lunch and then proceeded to climb, jump, and play on every piece of furniture that quickly became their imaginary pirate ship. Maxi, the oldest, taunted his younger sister, Connie, who bravely perched on top of a tower of chairs stacked ceiling high, swinging her makeshift sword and crying out, "I will take you prisoner!" The little one, Bangie, joined in her siblings' fun by running circles around the tables, including ours, swinging her wooden "dagger" and making menacing gestures towards her dad. The taverna was not busy since tourist season was long passed, so they had run of the whole place, and no one seemed to mind, least of all their parents, who kept a watchful but amused eye on them.

It wasn't long before I would witness this type of behavior in various forms from Greek children in many other local tavernas.

The only difference was that Mama would usually corral her child to shove another spoonful of *pastisio* (Greek macaroni and cheese) as he/she ran passed her. (The Greeks think their children never eat enough.) Although this kid chaos seemed to be acceptable in most Cretan tavernas, I could hardly imagine anything like that happening in America or heaven forbid, "rigid" Germany or "proper" England. Still, it *was* a casual beach taverna with very few patrons, and after sitting for two hours in a tiny church chair trying to make sense of all the foreign sounds, I was tempted to join them in their raucous, unbridled play.

This family ended up being an answer to my homesickness prayer because you couldn't be with them and still feel lonely. They opened their hearts and home to us, and we formed a friendship that still binds us together today through the years and over the miles. The taverna escapade was the first of many entertaining and joyous occasions we shared together. Any time we wanted to ramp things up in our lives, we paid a visit to the Kabutz clan and always departed with a smile and great memories. We jokingly refer to our first three months in Crete as baptism by fire, with the Kabutz family being the much-needed first responders.

Even if I wanted to sit around and lick my wounds of homesickness very long, Helene would hear nothing of it. She immediately zeroed in on my gifts as a musician and plunged me into her projects, which included a women's Bible study, music lessons for her children, and a summertime vacation Bible school day camp for children at her home. Her energy was topped only by her creativity, and she behaved like a woman possessed, which she was—possessed by her love for God. Our favorite story of our new friendship was when she announced to me in typical Helene style, "You are the answer to my prayers for a mentor!" After struggling with that ominous mission that most times felt like the proverbial square peg in a round hole, I finally sat her down after a few months and said gently, "I know you said God told you I was to be your mentor, but . . . I didn't get that memo." We laugh about that now, especially since another woman much wiser than me appeared in our lives shortly after. She was definitely more suited to the challenging assignment of mentoring Helene. We all agreed that although God didn't mean for me to be her mentor, He knew we both desperately needed a friend. And more than once, she reminded me that beauty can rise out of the ashes of loneliness.

My mood matched the gray weather and barren landscape. As I trudged along, I contemplated this wild, unpredictable place we now called home. It occurred to me that maybe I identified with this island more than I wanted to admit. Maybe the draw I had to it is that in many ways it reflected the condition of the human heart—a landscape of dichotomy. The cliffs loomed above me, drawing my gaze to their impossible heights and daring me to attempt to touch them. I knew their hard, unforgiving, unattainable peaks and gorges were filled with thorny, dangerous vegetation and the dry, sparse soil was full of craggy rocks and boulders. Yet those same cliffs and barren hillsides sloped down and

disappeared into the soft azure sea of the Mediterranean—a
liquid comforter—warm, receptive, inviting, playful and
at times cranky, but even that passes quickly.
It occurred to me that we mirror that same dichotomy in
our hearts. Sometimes hard and impenetrable and other
times gentle and accepting. But even the volcanic rock that
hasn't submitted to centuries of pounding waves—even this
rock has its redeeming qualities.
It's porous.
It accepts the water, soaks it in, and if there's any soil at all
hiding in its cracks, vegetation springs forth. So it is with
me.
I pray that even the hardest spots in my heart unsmoothed
by time and persistence, will be like volcanic rock—porous
and accepting of God's love. And from it, something good
will take root and bloom, giving color, beauty, hope and life
to the barren landscape.

Navigating the extreme differences in culture was always a
challenge that kept me on my toes. But I only had to observe an
"ugly American tourist" once to appreciate the virtue of tolerance.
It didn't take me long to recognize that Greece (especially Crete)
was not, and never would be, even close to America or western
Europe, so I would do best to remember to take it for what it
is. When I let go of my expectations and hang ups, I started to
appreciate Crete in a whole new way, seeing it with new eyes. It
took Richard a lot longer to get to that point. Even within the
first months of living there, he was looking forward to moving

back to the States, and I have to admit, there were days where I was ready for a one-way ticket home.

Theologian Dietrich Bonhoeffer wisely said, "It is in our securing things for tomorrow which makes us so insecure today." Our biggest challenge was resisting the temptation to look so far ahead that we failed to live in the moment. Perhaps that is the most valuable lesson I learned from living abroad. Living in the moment taught me to open my eyes, be aware, and be sensitive to everything going on around me. If I spent too much time nursing the "if only's" or pining about the "what if's," I would completely miss the breath of God on this one moment in time, the "Wow!" of now. If it's true that God inhabits every moment, then there's always something to smile about in every day. Sometimes you really have to look hard to find it. Other times it's just around the corner. All the time, it's there waiting for the observant wanderer with a grateful heart. Nothing breathes warmth and life into the heart of winter's discontent like gratitude . . . and as we soon discovered, a working fireplace.

BEYOND THE BEACH

"Endaksee" – a Greek word loosely translated as "It's all good," or "It's all right." A highly subjective reassurance. Endaksee usually means, "No problem," even if it's a big problem.

We are going on our fourth year of living here in western Crete with really no promising opportunities on the horizon for a job to return to in the States. When I realized we were going to be on the island for yet another wet winter, I decided it was time to get some things done that we'd put off. First order of business: a fully functional fireplace. In the previous winters, we tried everything to coax a fire out of the fireplace in our living space . . . without entirely smoking up the house. Last year, the landlord inspected the flue to make sure it was all clear, made a little fire, closed the glass door, announced, "Endahksee!" and then promptly left. Ten minutes later, I opened the fireplace door to stoke the fire only to be enveloped in smoke and soot. So this fall, we insisted on a fireplace expert who arrived with our landlord, and after a couple hours' work on the chimney, we were rewarded with a working fireplace. The chimney work also produced three charred bird carcasses, a giant nest, and all the metal contraptions that didn't work—which by the way, are still in our backyard after being haphazardly tossed down from the roof. Apparently, cleanup was not included in the service.

Surviving winter on Crete is just a matter of staving off that feeling of isolation called "rock fever" and keeping busy with what the island has to offer. Getting off the island is not only expensive during the winter months but inconvenient as well. The flip side is that the flights don't go the other way either, and so it's a perfect time to explore and experience without the crowds. Rainy season aside, winter on Crete can include some stellar weather. The trick is to get outdoors and enjoy what it has to offer.

So, here's our top ten, in no particular order:

1. Go up to Omalos and play in the snow.
2. Take advantage of the cooler temps and grab your bike to explore some amazing terrain around the Akrotiri, the Apokaronas, and the spectacular Therisso Gorge.
3. Take a hike in one of the numerous and spectacular gorges on Crete. The famous Samaria Gorge is

closed in the winter, but there are many others open, as well as hiking trails around the countryside.

4. Head up to Fournes, the orange capital of western Crete. You'll find roadside stands and stores filled with the sweetest of mandarins and oranges. And don't forget the fragrant lemons. Every self-respecting Greek cooks with lemons.

5. Stroll around the empty streets of Old Hania; check out the archeological ruins tucked back near "knife alley"; walk around the harbor and then grab a hot lunch of mouthwatering Cretan cooking at the hip taverna, Kouzina in Splanzia, a local favorite.

6. On a calm day, spend some time in the water (in a wetsuit!) paddleboarding and snorkeling at Marathi Beach or Stavros Cove.

7. On a windy day, go kite sailing at the big, beautiful beaches of Falasarna, Elafonissi, or Agia Marina.

8. Take a deck of cards (or use the in-house backgammon sets) and top off the day at KouKouVhia café set high above the city while you enjoy the best view of Hania at sunset in the company of friends over a steaming coffee and to-die-for chocolate dessert.

9. Grab some friends and spend the afternoon at a local winery like Manousakis or Dourakis near Hania. Or stay warm inside and out by sharing a cup of raki-infused tea around a beach fire.

10. On a blustery day, bundle up and go to the beach
    to watch God's thrilling show of force in the waves
    pounding the shore. Or on a nice day, just sit on
    the empty beach and soak in the quiet.

And on those winter days when the wind is howling and the
sideways rain is beating at your door, grab a cup of mountain
tea and a good book and count your blessings that you're not in
Chicago!

Not too many people deliberately book a vacation on Crete in
the winter, but I found it's the best time to really get to know the
island, explore, taste, and experience at a leisurely and deliciously
sublime pace. Sizzling summer is the perfect season for indulging
in anything that involves activities in or on the water, and you
won't want to venture too far away from it. But as beautiful as the
water is, there is so much more just beyond the beaches, and the
time to discover these treasures is during the relaxing and cooler
off-season.

When a winter storm sets down over the island, it usually
brings violent winds, sideways rain, and dramatic lightning. But
the storms are short-lived and reap amazing views of snow-covered
mountains in the south, double rainbows over the northern sea
accompanied by the crashing symphony of chaotic surf on the
shores. When the sun reappears, it's the perfect time to get out
and hike, bike, camp, or beach-comb.

After a particularly wet, windy couple of weeks in December,
we had a welcome break in the weather. The Lefka Ori mountain
range that had been wrapped up in dense cloud cover for almost

two weeks finally shed its packaging and revealed a mirage-like gift of astounding beauty—magnificent snow-covered peaks looming above Hania. A fine remedy for cabin fever was a day spent outside playing in the sun and snow, a winter's trek from seaside to mountaintop. We started our morning off with a walk on the beach at sunny Stavros cove just a couple of kilometers from our house. With camp chairs in tow and an ample supply of snacks we spent a casual hour wading in the cool water, taking in the cliff views, beachcombing for sea glass and listening to the quiet sounds of winter on the shore. The water was as still as a pond and as transparent as the sky. Its halcyon blues and greens glistened with each slight ripple in the smooth surface. It was hard to tear ourselves away from such serenity, but we were anticipating an afternoon romp in the water of a different form – snow.

The Greeks on the island would shake their heads at our excitement to get to play in the snow. When Richard showed a colleague some photos of us snowshoeing and skiing in Colorado, she visibly shivered and asked incredulously, "Why?!" Of course, you have to understand these people are in full winter gear starting around November (boots, scarves and heavy down coats) because the temps have dipped below 60 degrees.

We packed up and headed off up the winding road to the mountains outside of Hania. The 8000-foot snow-covered peaks of the Lefka Ori range beckoned us upward. We drove the road less traveled that snaked up and around the west side of the mountain and crested at the ridge where giant wind turbines stood sentinel on their perch. From here, the view south opened up to the Libyan Sea. The road descended to the Omalos Plateau in a secluded area, pristine with new fallen snow. Suddenly, the pavement abruptly disappeared under a high wall of snow where the snowplow had obviously had finished its day's work. We ditched the car there and hiked the rest of the way to the open high plateau.

Here was a different scene altogether than the morning's sea view a mere forty kilometers away. A large expanse of untouched white spread out before us and nestled in the valleys and rocks. Here and there stood a lone, leafless tree, its branches punctuating the wintry scene. A tiny, whitewashed chapel stood almost invisible against the snow. Deserted farm buildings dwarfed by the surrounding mountain peaks hunkered down into drifts. And all around us there was a hallowed silence.

Playing in the snow, taking photos and hiking through drifts gave us a ferocious appetite, and soon we were driving back down the mountain in search of a taverna that would be open this time of year. Not far outside of Hania but still in the hills, we pulled off at a roadside café in hopes of finding a hot meal. We were delighted to find the door open and a large family gathered around a corner table filled with mouthwatering food. As we entered the taverna, all heads turned and they couldn't hide their surprise at seeing a couple of non-Greek strangers in their sleepy little village at this time of year.

A man who looked like he might be the patriarch of the family stood up and welcomed us, explaining that he was the proprietor and his family was just eating their midday meal in preparation for opening for dinner. Not wanting to disturb them, we politely and regretfully excused ourselves and headed for the door. He stopped us and enthusiastically directed us towards a table.

"No problem. We make you good food." At this point, we were so hungry that a peanut butter sandwich sounded positively gourmet so we weren't going to argue.

We ordered up a plate of chicken souvlaki, potatoes, tzatziki, a winter salad and a carafe of crisp local white wine. He motioned to a woman, presumably his wife, and she hustled off to the kitchen. Then he and the rest of the family settled back into their lunchtime lounging. Any awkwardness we felt at being the only patrons in the place disappeared when our food arrived. Typically, service in a Greek taverna consists of taking your order, bringing the food and then leaving you alone to enjoy. This time was no different. We ate every bite and then sat back and reminisced about the day as we finished our wine.

Over an hour later, when we motioned to the owner that we were ready for the check, he nodded and then returned with a plate of thick Greek yogurt topped with quince marmalade and accompanied with a small pitcher of cold *raki* (moonshine that acts as a digestive when taken in small quantities). This gesture of a simple after-meal seasonal dessert is also typically Greek and always complimentary. He was in no hurry to give us the check, and we appreciated the long lag time to sit and rest. After a while and a couple of dice games of *Farkel*, we paid the pittance of a bill and bid our goodbyes to the family. They were still sitting at the corner table where we had found them over two hours before, and they didn't look like they were in any hurry to finish up; also very typically Greek.

On the way back to sea level we marveled at our unique opportunity to experience Crete at all altitudes and all seasons. Winter is the season when the bright green clover with its tiny yellow flowers carpets the olive groves and the wild thyme blooms pink and fragrant. The herds of sheep and goats provide a constant lullaby of tinkling bells and sad bleating. The skies are painted with storm clouds and rainbows. The empty beaches sport virgin sands and collections of shells washed up from the recent storms. These things and a bottle of good wine or hot cocoa shared between friends in front of a warm fire make you believe that there's nothing "off" about the off-season on Crete.

TREASURED SIGHTS AND HIDDEN GEMS

NORTH COAST ROAD TRIPS

Every chance we get, we explore our little part of the world and always manage to discover something new along the path . . . through grapevines and olive groves, past shepherds' huts and stone chapels, along rugged hillsides and soft sandy beaches, navigating through narrow streets to the bustling farmer's market. And when we stop for a moment to relax from all the sightseeing and learning, we indulge ourselves by finding a quiet cove where we can just sit still, read, reflect, and thank God for blessing us with each other, for old friends and new, and for creating another beautiful spot in this world to enjoy.

O n another quiet winter morning, we awoke to partly sunny instead of mostly rainy skies and decided to venture out and check out some sites off the Akrotiri peninsula. Our friends Reg and Daphne had recommended an archeological site called Aptera just south of Souda Bay, so the four of us jumped in the car and headed out.

Aptera was a Roman settlement built on top of ancient Minoan ruins and is still being excavated at present. The huge cisterns designed and built by the Romans for their water storage were impressive, and the maze of Roman baths were evidence of the important social ritual of communal bathing in their everyday lives. Because of the time of year, we had the place virtually to ourselves so we could explore the entire site without distraction. The ghost voices of this once-bustling metropolis were now silent, and the crunch of pebbles beneath our feet seemed deafening. We crested a small hill and stood at the rim of a newly excavated Roman theater. Although deserted on this particular day, there was evidence that work was in progress and much of the theater had been uncovered. But most impressive was the discovery of remnants of the Minoan culture (2000 BC) that established Aptera as an extremely important trading city in the Mediterranean. The excavation of temples, tombs, artifacts, and large stone Cyclopean walls were a testament to the sophistication and resolve of this city that once housed upwards of 20,000 inhabitants.

With our interest piqued and our car gassed up, we took off the next weekend to explore the peninsula that jutted out into our view west of the Akrotiri. The Roudopou Peninsula looked remarkably like a sleeping dragon when the setting sun disappeared behind its neck, and it beckoned us to venture out to its lair. The drive was only about thirty minutes west of our home, but once we exited the National Highway, we spent all day on the winding roads taking in the sights of the arid peninsula. Before heading up the high road that skirts the coast, we indulged in lunch at a fish taverna in the seaside village of Kolymbari. As is the norm, the proprietor ushered us back into the kitchen and opened the icebox to reveal the catch of the day. We picked out a smaller variety of fish that they prepared with loads of olive oil. After spending way too much time trying to pick out the bones, we washed it all down with ample bread, feta, and local white wine, and then headed out.

The road through the Roudopou peninsula precariously winds its way high above the seacoast revealing some jaw-dropping scenery over the Aegean Sea. Once in a while, a little bit of a shoulder is available to pull off on and take photos of the sea view and of chapels carved into rock or hanging on a cliff above the water. Of course, the whole time, Richard was lamenting that he wasn't on his bike and I was thinking, *What?! Are you crazy?!* (Most hard-core bikers are.) It really would have been a white-knuckle road trip if I hadn't been so distracted by the beauty of it all. Luckily, I was in a calm state of mind after first visiting the monastery Gonias at the base of the Roudopou just outside of Kolymbari.

Not long after our stop, we took a right turn that led us down to the sea and a secluded little spot called Afrata frequented by locals during the summer. Deserted now, we spread out our picnic lunch on the stone beach and mentally made note to return during the summer for some rewarding snorkeling. Hitting the road again after our lunch, we turned inland and pointed our noses west towards the other side of the peninsula. Around every turn the tight little road revealed open vistas over the sea on one side and hidden little chapels tucked into the stone hillside on the other.

Literally thousands of these stone chapels are everywhere on Crete. You see them in monasteries, in caves, in seemingly inaccessible deep gorges, along roadsides and even in back yards. Some are intricately decorated inside and others are simple and rustic. But all of them are kept very tidy and clean. Many of them are "name chapels," built in honor of a saint and used maybe only once a year on that name day. For example, all the chapels named after St. John (Agios Yiannis) would be opened on his name day, which is January 7th.

We stumbled upon one of these chapels during our road trip on the Rodoupou. Stone steps led up from the edge of the road past a giant gnarly tree that bore the sign, "Church of Agia Marina." We climbed up the steps to a cave that had been converted into a sweet little chapel with a white washed front and a wood paneled door. A bell tower loomed over the chapel like an old stone sentinel keeping watch over the locked and quiet church waiting its July 17th name day celebration.

Our trip across the peninsula dumped us out onto the west side and an interesting little beach spot called Ravdoucha. Not on the tourist radar, this tree-lined cove is home to a couple of fine tavernas and a pleasingly secluded beach area that boasts some dramatic rock formations making it ideal for snorkeling. A shallow breakwater area provides a secure place where small children and timid adults can wade safely as they gaze out over the gulf of Kissamos-Kastelli.

In the other direction from our house, Rethymno is a quaint port town east of Hania and only a 45-minute drive, so it quickly became one of our favorite day trips in any season. Although smaller than Hania, Rethymno has much of the same history with Minoan, Hellenistic, Roman, Venetian, and Turkish influences. It flourished under Venetian rule, and many of the town's most charming attractions are from that era.

Like Hania, the cobbled streets in the old historic section are mostly pedestrian. The imposing Venetian fortress that overlooks the sea on one side and the city on the other is one of the largest castles ever built (1573). The massive arched doorway is the entrance point for an enjoyable escape of wandering the ruins, studying in the museum or simply indulging in a picnic on the ancient stones overlooking the sea. The fortress is a hub of activity in the summer months where events and concerts are presented.

On a summer excursion to Rethymno, we dropped in on a beautiful little courtyard restaurant called Avli in the old historic quarter. Tucked in under a bougainvillea-draped awning on a cobbled alleyway, *Avli* (meaning "garden") is a cool respite from the hot summer sun of Crete. We lingered there, enjoying a complimentary glass of very good local wine and some easy conversation with the manager, Mixalis. He acquainted us with Avli's many offerings, which included not only a top rated restaurant but some beautiful lodging as well in a restored Venetian mansion. Being peak season, the price for a night's stay was too rich for our blood, but we vowed to give it a try during the off-season. Mixalis invited us to give him a call, promising to give us a room for a very discounted winter price.

Several months later, Valentine's Day rolled around and we took him up on his offer. When I made the phone call to him for reservations and attempted to help him remember who we were (the two Americans looking for shelter from the heat) and the afternoon we spent together on the patio (in July over glasses of wine and good conversation) and his offer (our choice of any Avli suites for €100) there was a moment of silence on the other end of the line. At first I wasn't sure how I could say all that in Greek, but he suddenly lit up on the other end and laughed, "Oh! The nice lady and the big man!" I decided to claim it and we booked the room. I hung up with a chuckle, thinking to myself, *Imagine that! Interesting what impressions we leave behind us.*

Perhaps what he meant by "nice" can be better described as my (sometimes overly) friendliness and a wide-eyed exuberance for learning about people and their culture. And my "big man" husband's 6'2" frame towered over most of the Greek population by at least a head (talk about a stand-out in the crowd.) In any case, we enjoyed a knockout gorgeous suite and a to-die-for sumptuous dinner at Avli for our Valentines weekend getaway.

On one particular visit to Rethymno, Richard and I, with two American visitors in tow, snooped around the tight little back alleys in the shadow of the Venetian- and Turkish-inspired architecture. We followed no map; just strolled leisurely, stopping to admire old doorways, to pet the occasional friendly cat, and to inhale sumptuous scents wafting from a tiny kitchen on Minoos Street. We peeked into an old Turkish mosque that was being restored, lounged at a sidewalk café near the lighthouse in the harbor, and walked under the original city gate arch, Megali Porta. In Platanos Square in the center of the old city, tucked in between a bustling café and an ice cream shop, we found the Rimondi fountain, a gift to the city during the 16th century from one of Rethymno's early Venetian governors. This fountain, on the site of an earlier Roman water source, still flows with clear, drinkable water, so we filled our water bottles before moving on.

The last stop of the day was in a tight old neighborhood where all sorts of arts and crafts, souvenirs, and treasures spilled out of the tiny shops on both sides of the pedestrian path. I entered a jewelry store and struck up a conversation with the woman behind the counter as I tried on a ring with a Greek key design. No sooner had I slipped it on my finger than we both noticed a curious movement under us. Suddenly her eyes widened and she grabbed my arm. *"Ela! Ela!"* (Come! Come!) She and pulled me out into the alley, yelling something in Greek to other shop owners.

The alley was already full of people spilling out of all the stores, and it was only when she let go of my arm that I noticed the ground moving beneath us, and a bewildering sense of vertigo. The earthquake only lasted a few seconds, and no damage was done, but I was more than ready get away from the old historic quarter before any ancient stones succumbed to aftershocks. I couldn't get the ring off my finger (and I quite liked it,) so I hastily paid for it and literally ran to the open parking lot.

Many months later, we visited the same shop and the shop owner's eyes lit up with recognition. She invited us to sit and have some tea and sweets as we shared some laughs over the experience. When I left her shop, she handed me a gift, a small necklace that matched my ring. To this day, I still wear my "earthquake" ring because it symbolizes the unexpected; not only the memory of the sudden movement of the earth beneath my feet, but more importantly, the kindness and generosity of a stranger.

The Greek people taught me that generosity was not just a kind action, but also a way of life, offered up to friends and strangers alike. They held loosely to their belongings, and I had to be careful many times about my compliments. I remember remarking casually to a neighboring farmer about how I loved his field of watermelons, and ended up with seven of them on my doorstep the next day. The Christmas season approached, and I was soon to discover even more open-handed giving by those who had considerably less than I did. And I also discovered that the season of giving was another excuse for a Greek-style celebration that involved simplicity, joy, and lots of food.

CHRISTMAS ON CRETE
ΚΑΛΑ ΧΡΙΣΤΟΥΓΕΝΝΑ! (MERRY CHRISTMAS!)

Christmas on Crete is a refreshing season of pleasant, laid-back celebration involving minimal decorations, thousands of costumed Santas, and food, glorious food. Conspicuously absent is the big push right before Halloween when big box stores in America unveil their plethora of pre-lit Christmas trees and animated lawn ornaments. (Am I the only one who feels a bad case of hyperventilation coming on when I enter Walmart at the end of October?)

In Greece, the big annual holiday is Easter (*Pascha*), and it is strictly a religious holiday that lasts for an entire week (Holy Week). Christmas is a distant second, with minimal decorations in the community. Our first December on the island, we noticed a single string of lights across the narrow street in the center of our village, a few unassuming door decorations, and a strange array of "climbing Santas" on various balconies and terraces. These Santas were skinny, deflated-looking versions of the big man in the red suit. He was precariously perched on the rungs of a hanging ladder with his bag full of toys. The fact that we saw him everywhere made me wonder if a container of them had washed up on the beaches of Crete that year.

Christmas in Greece lasts for twelve days from Christmas through Jan 6 (Day of Epiphany). In the bigger cities like our own Hania, the municipalities decorate sculptures and trees in the city as well as boats in the marina with just enough lights to fight off the winter doldrums. As Christmas approaches, feelings of anticipation heighten as holiday menus and festive events are carefully planned out.

One such event is the annual Santa Run; a fundraiser for disabled and needy children in the Hania area. This event attracts the entire young adult population and much of the older generation as well. When we ventured into the city during our first Christmas on the island, we were astounded by the mass of participants. From our vantage point on a balcony above the crowd we saw hundreds of Santa suits, hats, and white beards. They walked the narrow streets of Hania dancing and singing to blaring music. From above, it looked like a river of red lava slowly moving in one direction from the old harbor to the city hall. Occasionally, a group circled up, entwined arms, and spontaneously busted out a Greek dance.

Every year this event is the Greek version of a big street party, and by the finish, everyone feels great about contributing to a worthy cause—or maybe they feel great because of the victuals offered on every street corner along the way. Sponsors of the event and local shop owners provide tables of refreshments, but unlike the water stations in a typical American foot race, these tables are set with cups full of a different kind of water: firewater (*raki or tsikoudia*.) Either way, we discovered it's an occasion not to miss either as a spectator or a participant.

Later that week, we threw our own Christmas party and hosted over twenty-five people from six different cultures in our home. I stocked up on typical American holiday delights, and everything was a big hit, especially the glazed ham (which our Greek friends loved since it's not available in the local markets). We threw in some tasty international concoctions like *gluewein* (hot spiced wine) from Germany, figgy pudding from the UK, and a Cretan dessert specialty called *galaktoboureko*, a melt-in-your-mouth crackling filo pastry layered with rich cream filling and dripping with honey.

The evening stretched into the night, and since no one was in a hurry to depart, I grabbed my guitar and we all launched into a medley of Christmas carols. One thing led to another, and in the aftermath of many mugs of *gluewein* that fed the flames of creativity, we jointly composed our own version of *The Twelve Days of Christmas*. Between brainstorming and belly laughs, we realized that everyone has their own version of the Cretan experience.

THE 12 DAYS OF CRETE-MAS

On the first day of Crete-mas my true love gave to me:
   A goat in an olive tree
   Two loaded shotguns
   Three dumpster cats

Four herds of geep*
FIVE RAKI SHOTS*
Six Greeks a-shouting
Seven roosters crowing
Eight dogs a-barking
Nine Yia-yias* sweeping
Ten beat-up trucks*
Eleven fender-benders*
Twelve watermelons

* *Geep – A farm animal that looks like a cross between a goat and a sheep (i.e. not a pretty sight)*
* *Raki – Cretan moonshine*
* *Yia-yia – Greek grandma*
* *Usually old Toyotas that don't look any better than the donkeys they replaced*
* *You'd be lucky to get away with only eleven*

Christmas Eve was spent baking cookies with the Kabutz' six-year-old daughter Bangie, before heading off to Hania to take part in the Christmas Eve service at the International Church of Hania. We were part of the worship band made up of guitars, a keyboard, a small drum set, and a lot of different dialects. An exercise in simplicity, it boasted no extravagant production with lights, sound, and multimedia images bent on perfection; just a church full of diverse people who sang, prayed, and spoke the joy of Christmas into a small corner of this imperfect world.

By the time the service was over and we spilled out onto the sidewalks of Hania, the city was throbbing with energy. The mild night air was thick with holiday reveling. It was a perfect evening for a walk in the city. We ambled from the church down the streets and into the business center of Hania. In front of the main entrance of the *Agora* (indoor market), a 30-foot lit sculpture of a Christmas tree illuminated the face of every passerby. A few irreverent souls posed with the life-sized plastic nativity figures in front of the tree to snap a selfie.

Each corner of Hania was popping with activity and crowded with local partygoers. We stopped in for a late night snack at Kalamaki's - a small walk-up joint open to the sidewalk. There we ran into our good friend Nick and his daughter, Christina. Amidst the hubbub of noise and action going on around us, we shared a small table and some great conversation over grilled marinated meat on a small stick (*kalamaki*) and cold beers.

"You must join us for Christmas dinner tomorrow! Marina is cooking up some very special food. Delicious!" Nick smiled at his daughter who was nodding her approval.

Knowing the combined culinary talents of he and his wife, it took us only a New York minute to say, "Yes! What can we bring?"

"Bring your guitar." Nick, a music lover with the soul of a poet loved to hear me play and sing. I was more than happy to oblige, knowing it was the best way to show my appreciation for their gracious hospitality.

The typical household has traditional food for the holiday, just as we do in the States. However, it looks very different from our Christmas holiday fare. Our sugar cookies are replaced with an oblong-shaped cookie called *melomacarono*, which are made from flour, olive oil, honey, and cinnamon, and sprinkled with walnuts. While we bake up traditional pumpkin or spice breads, the Greek traditional Christmas bread is called *christopsomo* (Christ's bread). This round-shaped sweet bread is baked on Christmas Eve, and the sweet aromas of orange, cinnamon, and cloves permeate the house. The main meat on the Christmas table is usually lamb or pork slow-cooked in the oven or on the spit and accompanied by winter vegetables and seasonal salads.

The customary gift to take when invited to a meal in someone's home is usually "sweeties" or an elaborate dessert from one of the many fine shops called *Zacharoplasteion*, literally "sugar shop." Not to be confused with a bakery (breads and cakes), the sweet shops specialize in all types of candies, chocolates, cookies, and pastries. Each shop is intricately decorated with displays of tantalizing sweets that rival any French patisserie.

We entered one such shop on Christmas Eve to pick out a few sweets to take to Nick and Marina's home the next day. Resisting the urge to take one of everything, we picked a few chocolates, some honey-drenched baklava, and a dozen Greek Christmas cookies. The young lady behind the counter carefully placed them in a gift box and wrapped it up with an artistic flair complete with festive bows and ribbons. Only later did I find out that this treatment was standard for any purchase regardless of size or occasion. (I once walked into a sweet shop for a couple of cookies to eat on the run and walked out with a gift-wrapped box.)

This particular Christmas week was unseasonably mild, with the very welcome absence of the harsh winds that are normal for the winter months. The day after Christmas was a perfect day to get out and do some biking. Richard and I started out in Hania and headed west on the old highway that hugs the coastline. It was surreal to pass through the tourist hub of Platanias and see the hotels completely empty and the street almost deserted. The resorts were locked up and waiting for maintenance and repairs in preparation for the next onslaught of summer tourists.

Continuing west along the shoreline, we biked along the old runways of the now deserted World War II Allied Air Base in Meleme. Our trek ended at the fishing port of Kolymbari—a total of 23km one way. As we indulged in a much needed coffee and *spanikopita* (spinach pie), the other patrons regarded us with curiosity. By now, we were getting used to the stares of the locals (I guess two American gringos on bikes in the off-season deserve that), but we were always warmly greeted with Cretan hospitality wherever we went, especially on our bikes.

The week went by quickly with each day and night filled with friends and festivities. New Year's Eve was no different. Spirits were high all around the city. The kids were especially jazzed up because this day was the Greek Christmas Eve and they were anticipating a visit from St. Basil (Greek Santa Claus.) January 1 is St. Basil's Day, the day for gift exchanging and parties. During the afternoon we parked ourselves at a sunny table in a waterside taverna at the old harbor. Soaking up the sun, sipping our coffees, and listening to the Greek conversations around us was uncharacteristically relaxing for Americans at Christmas. A small group of youngsters approached each table singing songs accompanied by a triangle and hand drum. Sometimes they were given spare change. We noticed that the patrons were surprisingly tolerant and even encouraging of these little "beggars." When they approached our table I leaned into a friend and asked, "What is this about?"

She reached into her wallet for some small change for the children, "It's a custom this time of year for children to go from house to house singing carols called *kalandas* on Christmas and New Years Eve. It is expected to give them sweets or money in exchange for this blessing."

As evening approached, we walked to Nick's home where we had been invited once again for dinner. (They just couldn't seem to get enough of us – or maybe it was the other way around.) Our large group of friends and family squeezed around a long table in their small apartment and reveled in a sumptuous feast. Afterwards, we all waddled together down the street towards Hania's city center. Fireworks were popping and exploding all around us. Everyone seemed to have their own stash, and as midnight approached, the whole city pulsed with fireworks echoing out from back alleys and raining down from upper balconies.

As we approached the indoor market area, the mob scene was impressive and the party was just starting. Conspicuously absent were the police, which seems to be the case most of the year. But this was a jovial crowd with no ill intent and we felt perfectly safe. We ended the night with cries of *"Kali Kronia!"* (Happy New Year) to friends and strangers along the street and headed to our hotel room. Each New Years we treated ourselves to a nice hotel in Hania, and this year we took a room at Casa Delfino, a beautifully restored Venetian mansion near the old harbor.

Our Christmas in Crete was just one of many times we look back on and reminisce about good times. Crete in the winter is amazing. Yes, there is the occasional cold snap and sideways rain, but winter on the island is mostly known for its sleepy, relaxed way of life that chugs along happily. This is the season when the island enjoys cooler temps, no crowds, great hiking/biking weather, and every excuse in the world to hang out by the fireplace in a cozy taverna with friends and family. Plus, the sweetest of all fruits of this season busts out all over the island, and an excursion to a local orange orchard is just another way to beat the winter blues and come away with bags of sunshine.

THE WINTER GREENS
. . . AND ORANGES

In our village, the people tend to their farms and homes with a slower, relaxed pace—always taking time out for the afternoon siesta and making family the ultimate priority. Over the past twenty-five years, the economy in Greece has gone from bad to worse and every household here is affected. The men talk about it in the local "kafenios" over a cup of muddy Greek coffee or a shot of raki; families join together on a rooftop patio and complain (loudly) about their financial misfortune. With few exceptions, I see a real sense of community. Suffering is shared together as readily as a plate of biscuits and a coffee. Neighbors help each other. Families stick together. And friendships are nurtured like a slow stew on a winter morning.

Winter on Crete brings drenching rains with howling winds that whistle through the shutters and loosen the tiles on the roof for days at a time. And then, just when you feel like you're going to pull your hair out from the relentless noise, there's a break in the clouds and the Mediterranean sunshine chases the winter hooligans away and dispels any memory of nasty weather.

I awoke to one such morning in the dreary month of February. Thick gray clouds hovered over the distant mountains of the Lefka Ori in the south, and I wondered if it was still raining (or snowing) in the high hills. Looking north over the Aegean Sea there was a spectacular full double rainbow set against the dark clouds behind it. As I stood in a sunny spot by the window, I sipped my mountain tea infused with local thyme honey and absorbed the greenness of the landscape. In my hometown in Colorado, most winter days came in shades of brilliant white or drab brown under a canopy of piercing blue sky. The winter light cast shadows on the dark green pines making them look black in the distance. Spring green was nowhere to be found.

But in Crete, green was the color of winter. The dry brown earth of summer came alive in bursts of neon-green clover and vibrant wildflowers. How the earth managed to capture any moisture was beyond me, since most of the rain moved sideways. But the budding landscape reminded me that spring was around the corner, and until then I would do well to appreciate the wonders of winter on this island, one of the greatest being the ripening of citrus fruits.

There is nothing but goodness about winter in Crete when the citrus trees bear fruit, their branches heavy with juicy oranges, sweet mandarins, and fragrant lemons. An afternoon in the orchards was just another way to enjoy what Crete had to offer during its low season.

We were invited on our first "field trip" to the citrus orchards of Crete by one of Richard's colleagues from the Navy base. Katerina warmly welcomed us shortly after we set foot on the island, and in the ensuing years she became a close friend who always looked for opportunities to educate and engage us in the lifestyle of her homeland. A very intelligent young woman who was educated abroad, she could have opted to settle down in an engineering career anywhere in the world but instead chose to return to her roots and her family in Crete. They all live in Hania now, but her father's family originally settled in Modi, a tiny village in the hills outside of the city. At first blush, there doesn't seem to be anything particularly appealing about Modi. It is a sleepy little village that is hidden away down a long lane flanked by orange orchards. The village consists of a handful of old stone homes, a whitewashed church with an ancient bell tower, and a cemetery with a remarkable view over the hills of Crete. But the very simplicity of it oozes an uncomplicated type of charm.

One damp winter morning, Katerina met up with us in the village square next to the church and escorted us to her family's orange groves. She had warned us that the ground would be very wet and thick with undergrowth, but we weren't deterred. The lucky ones in our group owned tall rubber boots; the rest of us wrapped plastic bags around our shoes and stomped off into the trees. It wasn't long before exclamations of delight and laughter began to break out in our group as we filled our bags with the bright orange spheres of mouthwatering refreshment.

The sweetest of the oranges were the mandarins—a huge burst of goodness in a small package. Some brave souls climbed into the trees to collect the fruit at the top, but most of us were satisfied with the bounteous crop of fruit that tempted us at eye level. The trees were heavy with oranges, and their branches bent down low as if to invite us to relieve them of their burden. The fruit was dripping with moisture from the morning's rain, their dimpled skins glistening against the dark green foliage.

We kept our energy up by frequent samplings of vitamin C, and when our bags were brimming and heavy with fruit, we lugged them out to our cars. Looking behind us at the grove of trees, I was surprised to see how much fruit was still left on the branches. The only evidence that a group of hoarding orange pickers had been there was the flattened imprint of a dozen footsteps in the thick green clover that carpeted the orchard.

After the orange picking adventure, Katerina invited us to partake in a picnic of sorts that she had set up in her father's old family home in the village. The simple stone structure was now deserted, but the thick cement walls in the old house had seen plenty of action in its prime. Katerina entertained us with some of the history of this old house as we feasted on homemade *spanikopita,* fresh fruit, grape pudding, and a Greek-style power bar called *pasteli,* made with honey, various nuts, and sesame seeds. I didn't realize how hungry I was until I looked at the roughly spread lunch before us. But my appetite for more details about the house and her family wasn't satisfied until many months later when her father Stelios agreed to speak with me and fill in some blanks. Katerina acted as translator and we settled into the small living room after a ample supper prepared by her mother.

Stelios remembers when the German invasion of Crete during World War II brought unwelcome occupiers to their little village of Modi. Because of its close proximity to the British coastal airfield of Maleme, where the invasion started, it was one of the first villages to be subjugated to the German forces.

"I was ten years old when there was a knock on the door. A tall German commander stood in the doorway. He informed my parents that their home would be needed as a headquarters. We were afraid because we didn't know where we would live. Many villages had seen families on the streets after being thrown out of their homes. But this commander was kind and he permitted us to stay in our two-room home. From 1941–1944 we lived in one room with only a wall between our occupiers and us. We were one of the few fortunate villages on the island."

While many other villages suffered the cruelties of war, including executions and homes being burned to the ground, Modi was fortunate to have a German commander with a respect for and interest in Greek culture. During the war, it was a common practice for many Cretan villagers to be deported to Germany as slave laborers, and they were never seen again, but the German commander saved Modi by not permitting any deportation from the village. He showed his kindness in other ways as well.

"I remember when the commander requested that each man in the village provide a horse for him to ride. When my father gave him a horse, he admired the commander's saddle, and remarked to him, 'It is very beautiful.'"

"The commander told my father, 'One day, when I don't need it anymore, I will give it to you.' The day before the Germans evacuated the island, he sought out my father and, true to his word, he presented to him the prized saddle."

Katerina's grandmother, Yia-yia Stella, was sitting next to Stelios, her son-in-law, and listened intently. I had the sense that she had stories of her own to tell.

"Yiayia Stella, what do you remember most about your childhood?" I asked.

She smiled faintly at me and replied, "I remember in 1941 I was 13 years old. My parents hid my younger sister and me in nearby caves to find safety during the German invasion of World War II. That was a very hard time, because we were so frightened. My sister kept crying, and I had to tell her to be quiet. And we were so poor—no food," she added gazing off.

But even in the midst of war and poverty, the Cretan communities came together and continued to work, dance, sing, and fall in love. She and her husband, Manolis, were childhood friends from the same village and were married when they were both very young. Her mood lightened and her eyes shone when she talked about him.

"Manolis would buy raffle tickets for each of our children, but not for me because, he would say with a wink, 'She already won the prize – ME!'"

Stella is now 90+ years old and moves with a slow and careful shuffle, but her blue eyes sparkle when she tells that story and her smile is one of a much younger woman.

She was once a great singer, and at the end of an evening spent with this special family I asked her to sing me a song. She shyly smiled and hesitantly began singing the first few notes of her favorite song, *To Kanarini* (The Canary). As her voice lifted in confidence, she serenaded us, singing each verse in her soft Cretan dialect. I knew I was witnessing something precious—her gift of music offered to me—and in that moment, there was an unspoken understanding between us. The simple gift of a song had the power to transcend culture and time.

SPRING

Spring on the island of Crete is like no other place on earth. The long, hard winter rains yield a landscape profuse with wildflowers and greenery. The island wakes up from its restless winter slumber and wastes no time in decking itself out in the happy attire of spring. Fields are adorned with bright little heads of red poppies, delicate purple bell flowers, and pale pink, fragrant wild roses. Along the roadside and towering above fences stately yellow fennel sway in the gentle breeze. Small bright-faced anemones decorate backyards everywhere, carpeting the grass with the colors of purple, pink, and white. The sky is a happy shade of blue with few clouds, and the sea dances gently on the shoreline as if in anticipation of more visitors.

Spring brings out the promise of rejuvenation to the island.

Local farmers begin planting their summer crops, including plump Cretan tomatoes, juicy cucumbers and blushing sweet watermelons kissed by the sun. Little white lambs frolic around the fields, oblivious to their fate come Easter week. Beekeepers don their protective clothing and inspect their hives, a practice dating as far back as their Minoan ancestors. The village women combine their efforts to begin some serious spring housecleaning, sweeping, washing, and wiping down their terraces in anticipation of moving their meals outdoors under the sweeping bougainvillea vines.

Spring brings change . . . new life from the dust, new color to a gray world.

The island begins to hum with anticipation of its major events: planting for a new harvest, preparing for tourist season, and celebrating the most important of Greek holidays—Easter, or *Pascha*. Whole villages busy themselves with preparations, including slapping whitewash paint on everything that doesn't move out of the way, from their homes to their stone walls to even the rocks and tree trunks that line the side of the road.

Spring brings hope.

Hope for a more abundant harvest and a more profitable year.

Hope for dreams realized and lives reinvented.

WEEDS AND WILDFLOWERS
THE EYE OF THE BEHOLDER

I'm sitting in a shady spot on a stone wall in the Agia Triada monastery courtyard. After the short, easy 15-minute bike ride to this peaceful green oasis, I ponder why I don't do this more often. I've been here too many times to count, but usually on a nice warm day the sea beckons me and I find myself on the beach. Instead, today I find my favorite shady spot at a monastery to write and reflect. Potted flowers and herbs, blooming fruit trees, and cheerful birds surround me. And, of course, there's always a stray cat (or ten) looking for a lap to sit on.

Warmer weather descended on the island, and our outings became more frequent. One such outing was in the hills outside of Hania. *Agia Kyriaki* is a former seventeenth-century monastery with an intriguing history. When the Turkish occupation was at its height during the nineteenth century, it served as a haven for refugees and freedom fighters. Now owned by the nearby monastery *Chrisopigi*, it is the quiet and hospitable home of about twelve nuns.

We left our car in the dirt parking area under the olive trees, and rang the little doorbell of the small convent. A sweet-faced nun opened the door and greeted us with a soft spoken *"Kalimera. Kalo Oriste."* (Hello. May I help you?)

"May we come in?" I indicated.

"Nai, fysika!" (Yes, of course.)

She offered us a cup of cold water and motioned to another nun in the courtyard to join us. The other nun approached us with a smile and a slight bow and said in perfect English, "Hello. Welcome!"

I was delighted to know we could relax and speak in our mother tongue with this friendly nun.

"My husband and I are living in Hania and heard about Agia Kyriaki from a Greek friend. She told us we must visit this place and now I can see why. It's really beautiful here, so peaceful and serene."

I looked around the small courtyard filled with flowers, herbs, and a large but sweet dog that looked to be as old as the stones in the building. He sauntered up to us and happily received his pats.

With a twinkle in her eye, she motioned to the dog. "That's Argus." I thought to myself, *How appropriate.* Depending on which myth you chose, Argus was either a hundred-eyed monster or the aged faithful dog of Odysseus. This old creature standing before me in perfect tail-wagging submission was definitely the latter.

Our hostess invited us to enter into the small gathering room equipped with rustic wood furniture and a long table set with pure white linens and a centerpiece of cut flowers from the garden. The scene was charming, and I felt the urge to hide in its silence for a while, but the day was approaching the noon lunch hour.

As we walked through the courtyard, we enjoyed easy conversation fueled by genuine interest in each other's lives. The nun showed us to the door and before we left, offered us a booklet written by her, about practicing the Greek Orthodox faith at Agia Kyriaki. When we walked out the convent door, she called after us.

"Don't forget to visit the gardens. Just continue up the path."

We promised we would, and with a smile and a wave, she closed the large wooden door behind us.

The long walk up the stone path revealed small doorways tucked under overhangs in the rock cliffs. Most of them were locked, but we found one that opened into a musty, dark room. As our eyes adjusted to the lack of light, we realized it was a tiny cave decorated with whitewashed walls and rustic religious ornaments. These chapels were tucked away into an ecosystem that had been painstakingly honored through the cultivation and care of the surrounding gardens. In the distance, we could see the main convent through the trees. It sat like a golden beacon on the hill at the top of an ever-ascending stairway.

As we strolled up the cobblestones, we remarked how this place was like an oasis in a frantic city. Our cares evaporated away on the cool breeze scented with the aromas of the impending spring. Wild herbs grew along the path and in sunny spots under the blooming olive and almond trees. I tilted my head back, and inhaled the intoxicating sweet and earthy scents of blooming thyme, sage and rosemary. Not to be outdone by the herbs, the wildflowers popped their sweet heads through the green grass and shouted with vibrancy. Purple, pink and white anemones shared their space with yellow daisies and dainty redheaded poppies.

Crete introduced me to a whole new world of plants and herbs. At least it was new to me. For centuries, the islanders gathered many of the wild plants and "weeds" for cooking and medicinal purposes. Even today, the local pharmacies offer many alternative remedies from botanical plants. The rare dittany plant found in gorges and ravines is the main ingredient for a tea touted as a cure for any ailment. *Malotira Tea*, sweetened with wild thyme honey, became my favorite winter morning potion.

The fields and valleys of Crete yield abundant wild superfoods. In the spring and the winter, village women hike up their skirts and go into the fields and along roadsides to gather a particular kind of "weed." *Horta* is a common dish in Crete of boiled seasonal greens flavored with olive oil and lemon. Sometimes it's served cold like a cooked salad, but I preferred it warm with a bit of vinegar and sea salt. Depending on the variety of greens, horta can taste anywhere from bitter to sweet. But one thing all horta has in common is its vitamin-packed goodness. Another secret of the Mediterranean diet.

The magic of Cretan flora comes alive in a visit to the Botanical Park & Gardens of Crete outside of Hania. The gardens were the brainchild of four brothers from the village of nearby Skordalou. A devastating wildfire in October 2004 destroyed the entire region around the village. More than 60,000 olive trees were burnt to the ground and threatened the ruin of the village. But out of the ashes rose a vision: the first botanical park of Crete.

The four brothers of Skordalou hatched an unusual plan. Rather than replant the olive and orange groves, they designed a park dedicated to the preservation of indigenous plants and trees of Crete. The result was a preserve for botanical species and a center for environmental education. Litter, waste and dumping (coined as Cretan cancer) are common occurrences, especially in the rural areas. But thanks to visionaries like these brothers, many school children and adults are learning the value of taking care of their extraordinary island.

The botanical gardens are arranged on a series of terraces that boast a variety of ecosystems, from high tundra to the low tropics. The path zigzags its way along the steep hillside through displays of both rare and common plants found in the wilds of Crete. But the best part of a visit to this special area is the lunch at the taverna's stone patio, perched high on the side of the terraced gardens. The kitchen produces mouthwatering dishes with fresh ingredients grown on-site. We often took visitors there for a taste of Crete accompanied by a magnificent view.

One person's weeds are another person's wildflowers. It all depends on how you look at it.

The rains of winter yielded some of Crete's finest masterpieces. Wildflowers graced the meadows and mountains. In the early days of spring, I spent hours out in the fields with my camera capturing the color around our house before the farmer's plow arrived. But my most memorable spring excursion was a hunt for the elusive Cretan orchid.

Up until that day, my image of an orchid was limited to those large white or purple varieties that frequent the florists' section of grocery stores right before Mother's Day. The day had started out with a light drizzle as a group of us threaded our way up into the hills above the village of Spili. As we entered the high meadow, the wild tulips boasted their presence with prolific color, but the orchids were much more elusive. These shy little flowers hid from the untrained eye and could be easily crushed underfoot. Most of them were a mere 6″ high and grew in secluded niches and crevices.

The rare Cretan orchids are sought after by flower enthusiasts from all over the world. Just like cloud shapes, each orchid is unique in its detail. I discovered one that looked like a baby face with big ears. Another one looked like a Greek man with a white beard. Still another was the image of an angel holding a star. The only similarity between the orchids was their tiny, intricate design, each holding a story of the diversity of creation.

Gardening has always been one of my loves. Life itself is revealed in the cycle of new birth, growth, blossoming, bearing fruit, and seed, decaying and finally death. This cycle repeats over and over again—the promise of hope, restoration and revelation.

A spring walk along the beach with my Greek friend, Eri, revealed another Cretan gem. We were simply enjoying the sunshine, the warmth of the sand between our toes and a few laughs in each other's company. Suddenly, she stopped, bent down and gently cupped a small white flower growing straight out of the dry sand. Its delicate petals of translucent white blended so well with the sand, I had missed it.

"Sand lilies," Eri explained in her broken English, "They grow straight out of dry sand, not near water, yet they are born and given life by God." She remarked that these are the same lilies that Jesus saw in his Mediterranean surroundings and talked about in the Gospel of Matthew,

And why worry about your clothing? Look at the lilies of the field and how they grow. They don't work or make their clothing, yet Solomon in all his glory was not dressed as beautifully as they are. And if God cares so wonderfully for wildflowers that are here today and thrown into the fire tomorrow, he will certainly care for you.
So don't worry about tomorrow, for tomorrow will bring its own worries. Today's trouble is enough for today."
(Matthew 6:25-34)

Treasured memories begin with living in the moment. By opening my eyes to what seems small and insignificant, I increase my capacity for joy. The most vivid memories are born out of completely spontaneous and unexpected moments. These moments, laced together by the sights, smells and sounds of the Divine, reach down and touch the soul.

Sometimes they are like weeds born out of pain, suffering and trials.

Sometimes they are like wildflowers, an accidental joy in the unforeseen.

Today is a glorious spring day and the blue sky against the church's white dome looks like a postcard. A Greek Mediterranean island in the spring sounds so romantic. It is . . . sometimes. But Crete isn't untouched by the perils of this world. As with any romance, there are highs and lows, beauty and ugliness, weeds and wildflowers. No place this side of heaven is perfect. A friend once observed that this island is a harsh place to live and it will break you if you allow it. She meant this in a good way. We've all been through a romance at least once in our life that was worth pushing through the trials, painstakingly peeling back the stubborn layers to finally reveal a sweet fruit. It takes time, patience, tolerance, compassion, humility and a huge sense of humor.

But in the end it's worth it, because even weeds have their purpose.

PETS AND VETS

"When you do a thing, do it with all your might.
Put your whole soul into it. Stamp it with your personality.
Be active, be energetic, be enthusiastic and faithful
and you will accomplish your object."

—Ralph Waldo Emerson
Nineteenth-century American writer

Over the years of living on the island, we grew accustomed to the constant challenge of navigating many unfamiliar learning curves; curves that took surprising twists and turns—from adjusting to the chaotic to accepting the bizarre. But one thing I could never adjust to or accept were the poor and sickly stray cats and dogs that overpopulated the island. Their disturbing presence was a daily reminder of our responsibility as humans.

Most of the cats hung around dumpsters and were usually successful in scavenging for scraps of food. But in the rural areas, many of the dogs (dubbed "barrel dogs") were chained to 55-gallon steel drums for shade, which in the hot summer months acted more like an oven. These dogs existed on a token amount of food scraps and water. They lived out their miserable short lives as neglected guard dogs, preventing sheep from straying too far down the road. Not surprisingly, the life expectancy for Cretan stray dogs is two years and for cats, a pitiful six months.

Over the years, a few compassionate expats and Greek vets strive to provide care for these unfortunate animals. But, many locals oppose this effort. Fear of disease and sheer numbers are a concern; and in the case of cats, the unquestionable reality that wild felines can be a nuisance. Stray taverna cats prey on the sympathies of unknowing, softhearted tourists, much to the annoyance of the taverna owners. I admit, I have fallen victim to their pathetic meows and sorrowful green eyes as they sit under my feet hoping for a bit of calamari thrown their way.

With the daily evidence of the stray animal population around me, I was motivated to do my small part. I first learned of the local animal rescue effort through a friend. Sharon was a feisty red-headed American lady with a fireball personality and a heart of gold. She hosted veterinarians from Germany and England who traveled to Crete on their own dime, to work with the stray animal population on Crete with the help of dedicated locals and expats.

My first experience helping with the effort was an eye-opener. It began with combing the neighborhoods and searching community dumpsters. Over the next five days, we trapped cats and coaxed stray dogs into kennels to transport back to the clinic. The vets set up and manned a sterile and efficient environment where they provided medical care for the strays, including vaccinations, spaying, and neutering.

Sharon first approached me with a very convincing plea for help.

"It's only a weekend of your life, and you could make such a difference in the lives of these poor creatures. We NEED you!"

"OK," I agreed. "But I'm more comfortable working around dogs than cats."

"No problem," she said with a grin. "I'll put you in the post-op dog room. All you need to do is make sure they're comfortable as they come out of anesthesia."

I have to say this went remarkably well, and I was just starting to feel comfortable when she summoned me to the dreaded "cat room."

"Melanie, get in here!" she yelled, "NOW!"

When I entered the small room, Sharon and another volunteer were attempting to transfer a cat from the live trap cage into a holding cage for anesthesia. He was the biggest, meanest, wildest cat I'd ever seen, and he was absolutely pissed off at the world. It took three of us to maneuver him to a point where the transfer was almost complete. To this day, I'm not sure what happened next. All I remember was a 30-pound demon-possessed ball of filthy fur suddenly loose in the room, and I was ducking for cover behind Sharon. I never would have believed a cat could climb up a 7-foot glass sliding door if I hadn't seen it with my own eyes.

Honest to God, this huge cat went from the floor to the ceiling by scrambling up a pane of glass. I would have made my exit right then and there, but I was afraid to open the door. This beast had supernatural powers to do anything, including escaping through a crack in the door. So I flattened myself in a corner and tried to look invisible. I hunkered there and watched in amazement ats Sharon donned a pair of gigantic protective gloves that looked like something you'd see in a radioactive lab. She knew this was war and was determined to be the victor. The demon cat ran frantic circles around the room before she cornered it. It let out a hair-raising snarl and a howl as she grabbed it by the scruff of its neck and shoved it into the waiting cage.

I looked at Sharon with extreme admiration and silently dubbed her "the cat exorcist."

For days, the volunteers and veterinarians put in long hours caring for each animal. Sometimes we felt like we were swimming upstream. The clinics were always exhausting work because the need was overwhelming. But we continued to repeat them each year, knowing that we were somehow making a difference. A few well-behaved animals were adopted by waiting owners in Germany or the UK, a happy ending for a dog or cat whose days were certainly numbered on Crete. We experienced this process first hand with a Christmas surprise in 2010.

On Christmas Eve that year we stood on our rooftop terrace enjoying a balmy evening view of the sea. The serene evening was suddenly interrupted by the sound of frantic cries of some wild animal. We followed the sound to our front gate and discovered a frightened, flea-infested five-week-old puppy. Someone (not Santa) had dropped it over our security gate. Because it's not an uncommon practice for softhearted expats to be the unwitting recipients of unwanted animals, I was surprised we didn't get a whole litter. She looked like a yellow lab with caramel-colored fur and white smudges on her forehead, her toes and the tip of her tail.

Our initial annoyance and irritation melted away as we looked into her sweet brown eyes. Begrudgingly, we accepted that we were now the unsuspecting owners of a Cretan mutt. She had successfully adopted us. We took her in, gave her a bath, picked off the fleas, and set up a makeshift bed in a box. She settled in quickly, and as she fell asleep we sat back and scratched our heads about what to do with her. My sweet husband gave me that sideways look, let out a big sigh and said, "You want to keep her don't you?" I didn't see an option, since the shelters were overcrowded and no one wanted a puppy. We toyed with a gamut of names and finally settled on *Ela*, which in Greek means, "Come!"

For eight months she grew into a sleek, lively, friendly Cretan hound with more energy than a hive full of bees. Despite serious training, she never lived up to her name and ignored our commands to "Come!" It wasn't long before this pup of ours exerted her independence and lust for wandering. She grew bigger and stronger and began scaling our 6-foot stone wall in search of the nearest sheep herd to traumatize with her tireless game of chase. More than once I rescued her from the consequences of a loaded shotgun at the end of a local sheepherder's arm.

After a close call, we made the difficult decision to put her up for adoption in Germany. We knew her days were numbered in Crete and it was for her best. The heart-wrenching day came and I said goodbye with a kiss to her sweet face.

We missed her every day afterwards, but the hardest part of letting her go was not knowing her fate. About two weeks later, I received an email from her adoptive family. They had a big yard and two young, equally active children. A photo of her sound asleep beside her boy accompanied the email. She had found her home.

No sooner had we settled back into a more quiet and predictable lifestyle when another needy mutt rocked our world. This time it was a "barrel dog" (minus the barrel) tethered to a post and left with no food, water, or shelter. He was a mid-sized mass of gray and white matted fur that resembled a sheep dog. He was also a trusting and friendly dog with impeccable manners and the patience of Job. We rescued him, took him to the vet clinic and had him examined and vaccinated. After two hours of cutting off the mats of dreadlocks, my hands were a mass of blisters but the reward was a decent-looking Cretan mutt.

He looked suspiciously like a crazy character out of a Dr. Seuss book so the name stuck. *Seuss*. He was the antithesis of Ela. Whereas Ela was a hyperactive spaz case, Seuss was as excitable as a doormat. He was the most calm, laid back, chill dog I'd ever seen, but he came to life when it was time for a walk—with or without me. He suffered from the same syndrome that we saw in Ela. I called it the "Cretan Mutt syndrome"—that defiant attitude to run amuck on their own terms. More than once he took off, only to show up hours later sporting a look of complete satisfaction, and a grin that seemed to say, "I'm home! Did you miss me?" I could only imagine the trouble he got himself into. But he was a lovable old chap, so when we left Crete, we felt relief to find a good home for him on the island. The last time we saw him, he was the guest of honor at a BBQ, relishing in the attention of five American sailors and the meat scraps they threw to him.

Of the many things I miss about Crete, I will never miss seeing poor animals suffer from disease and hunger because of neglect or abuse. But I have seen the good side of humanity in many people on the island who make a difference in the lives of these animals. Compassionate Greek veterinarians and animal lovers are doing their part. They are fighting a noble uphill battle against overwhelming odds. And so I end with a happy story.

Two abandoned kittens, a scrawny male and his sister that were near death, stumbled into our yard. We took them to our local vet in Kounoupidiana, thinking they would probably need to be put down. But Stavros, Costas, and their staff examined the kittens and gave us hope. We left with medicine, care instructions, and two kittens with a second chance at life. After a week of nursing and loving on them, the kittens were strong and lively. But Seuss didn't appreciate the competition. So, Stavros and Costas stepped in again and helped us find good homes for two healthy, robust kittens.

I'm reminded of the Sand Dollar Story:

An old man was strolling along a beach one day. In the distance he saw a young boy and girl reach down, pick something up and throw it back into the sea.
Drawing nearer, he saw that the sand was littered with thousands of small stranded sand dollars. The children were

*patiently picking them up, one at a time, and returning
them to safety below the water.*

*"What are you doing?" he asked.
"Saving sand dollars," replied the children as they continued
about the job at hand.*

*The old man, somewhat jaded by age, thought the children's
actions were futile.*

*"But the beach is littered with dying sand dollars. What
possible difference can you make by doing this?"*

*The young girl bent over, picked up another, and threw it
with all her might. With a plop the sand dollar sank safely
below the water. Then, turning to the old man, she said
with all the wisdom of a child:*

"It made a difference for that one."

Two kittens here; a few dogs there. How do you make a
difference against the overwhelming odds?

One at a time.

SAVORING THE SWEET MOMENTS
VILLA KERASIA

"**L**et's see where this road goes."

Richard's words were music to my ears, since I'm not one to stick to a plan; and as it turned out, it was a good choice.

We were riding our bikes in the hills of a rugged yet serene area known as the heart of Crete's wine country. The hilly landscape was challenging but exhilarating as we peddled up grueling ascents and breezed down into the valleys below. This region in the midsection of Crete, south of the capital city of Heraklion, is known for its numerous and prolific vineyards that flow down the hillsides in perfect symmetry. The scenic beauty along quiet meandering roads make it perfectly suited for viewing from the saddle of a bicycle.

The barren road continued to ascend along the base of the Psiloritis mountain range. A ribbon of pink oleanders stitched the landscape together between remote hillside villages. Ano Asites, Nisi and Krousonas, villages solid with age and history, rooted themselves into valleys and on hilltops.

We planned to stick to the paved roads weaving in and out of villages and olive groves. But we had lived in Crete long enough to know not to trust the map. Instead, we meandered our way through the hidden villages in an attempt to make a big loop and discovered that going off the beaten path usually leads to the unexpected. Sometimes it ends with a dreadful surprise—like finding a dead end at the big hill you just *descended*. But other times, it can lead to a sweet, spontaneous moment. We had our share of both.

We happened upon a small chapel hidden among some trees and stopped to take a photo. Three men sitting in the chapel's courtyard waved at us and shouted, *"Ela, ela!"* ("Come here, come here!) We shrugged at each other and thought, *Why not?!* We made our way down to where they were taking a break after cleaning the grounds around the building. They greeted us warmly and we attempted our awkward Greek/English introductions. To our surprise, they insisted on sharing their simple lunch with us— grilled lamb, village bread, and fresh oranges.

We hurdled the language barrier with elaborate hand gestures, genuine smiles, and lots of shrugging. I couldn't understand some of their Greek verbiage, but I had a sneaking suspicion it had something to do with the American man in skin-tight latex. One man reached out and offered us each a cup of *raki* (Cretan moonshine*)*, which no self-respecting visitor can decline. I suspected they were testing Richard's level of machismo (very Greek), and to Richard's credit he didn't bat an eye.

Politely excusing my meager sip, they insisted Richard join them in a proper toast. (About this time I had visions of scraping Richard and his latex off the pavement down the road.) Not one to lose face, he accepted a cup, and under the watchful eyes of his new Greek man-friends, took a gulp (or was it two?) of the potent spirits. They each threw down a swig, followed by exuberant back-clapping. Their approving nods and cheerful guffaws told us he passed some sort of test. But I noticed that when they turned away from him, he discreetly watered a plant with the rest in his cup. Wise choice, since the day's heat was upon us and we still had miles to go. Saying our goodbyes, we peddled on towards the monastery of *Gorgolaini*.

The long shadows of the late afternoon lay across the serene monastery. We entered the pristine courtyard and rested on a cool stone bench under the shade of a giant plane tree. Plump plums hung from some trees in the orchard, and spring vines boasted reds and pinks. The silence was almost as refreshing as the cold water from the courtyard fountain.

Back on our bikes, we descended the hill from the monastery and noticed the village of Ano Asites in the distance. Passing through the village, we discovered a tiny church, Agios Antonios, at the top of a deep gorge. The gorge emptied out into the fertile valley below, where patchwork fields stood in the sun. As we took in the view from our perch on a stone wall, we marveled at how much more we saw and experienced from the saddle of a bicycle as opposed to the seat of a car. Exhausted and grateful, we made our way to our final destination. The perfect home away from home – Villa Kerasia.

Villa Kerasia drew us in the minute we stepped over its threshold. We began to feel layers of stress peel off with every step on the stone walkway leading up to the front yard where the view opened up to the expansive valley below. A long table was set under grape-laden vines, and a single pomegranate tree shaded the pool area. A most welcoming sight. But by far, the best greeting was the warm *"Yaisas!"* and genuine smile from Babis. He invited us to sit with him on the terrace.

While we cooled off over a glass of chilled Kerasia Rosé with a hint of cherries, Babis gave us some history of the renovation of the villa. The old villa, dated from 1883, was in a sorry state of crumbling walls and caved-in roofs when he first laid eyes on it. He was a boy then, living in a nearby village. Travels and education took him abroad but he always remembered the old villa. When he returned to Crete, he purchased the site and over the years lovingly restored it to a chic and comfortable bed and breakfast. Artistic touches indigenous to the culture of Crete decorate every nook and cranny of the villa. The large living room has space for everyone to relax, including the ever-growing population of kittens that roam outside, and sometimes inside, the house.

The next day we spent by the pool, reading and conversing with other guests. One guest in particular, a 70+ man named Mike, invited us to join him for yoga before breakfast. We realized he was in a league of his own, as he began doing yoga moves that we couldn't even think about attempting. We opted out of yoga and decided on breakfast instead. A full meal greeted us in the dining area. The table was laden with meats and cheeses, breads, and seasonal fruit, homemade jams, and Greek yogurt. The house specialty was sunny-side-up eggs floating in a pool of green, peppery, extra virgin olive oil from Babis' groves. Georgia, Babis' chef extraordinaire, made magic in the tiny but efficient kitchen.

That night, a feast of spectacular Greek cuisine and wine was set on the terrace. And the dessert was almost as sweet as the storytelling and laughter that accompanied it. The conversations around the table were laced with descriptions of off-the-beaten-track places to explore further into the hills and remote villages of central Crete.

The atmosphere of Villa Kerasia dares you to leave its sanctuary. But it's also the perfect place to set up home base from which to venture out and explore more of what this area has to offer. Each time we visited Villa Kerasia, Babis sent us off on our day trips with good directions of where to go, who to see, and what not to miss—and always the advice to keep our eyes, and our hearts, open.

I've come to believe that travel is a microcosm of life in general, an ever-changing experiment of adaptation. Some manage their lives like traveling without an itinerary. Grab a backpack, head out on the path, and see where it leads you. Others manage their lives like a well-executed road map. Point A to point B with all the stops between neatly planned. But both approaches have the guarantee of abrupt interruptions, joy or calamity. Life's sudden unexpected bumps in the road can be either deterrents or opportunities. It all depends on how you look at it. Interruptions can be blessings in disguise. Or at the very least, a great adventure that dares us to adapt and change for the better.

Living in the balance between the Here and the Beyond requires intention, courage and large doses of curiosity.

BEYOND KERASIA

THE HANDICRAFT VILLAGES OF ANOGIA, KOUSSES, AND THRAPSANO

Venturing up into the mountains of Crete always reveals a hidden gem or two of the "real" Cretan lifestyle. We set out one morning on a road trip with our fellow day-trippers Rolf and Marion Berger. The Bergers were Germans who were transferred to Crete for Rolf's job with the German Air Force. We became fast friends, and between Rolf's love for driving, Marion's love for cuisine, and our love for adventure that combined both, *Berger's Drive and Dine Adventures* was born.

Heading south from Heraklion, we left the main highway and opted instead for the winding roads through the mountains. Our first stop was at a tiny mountain village called Kousses located north of Matala. The small houses in the village clung to the hillside above a spacious valley. We were looking for a local shop we'd heard about called *Botano*. This first-rate establishment gathered and distributed locally grown spices and herbs to loyal patrons all over the world. This obscure but quaint little shop sat on a steep hillside, its front door right on the street and its back door opened to a balcony suspended high above the valley below.

Upon entering the small doorway, it seemed as though this very small space contained the contents of the entire ambrosial world. Large glass jars containing herbs and spices, lotions and soaps, lined every wall. The smell was intoxicating, and we meandered through the tiny shop marveling at how many things one can create from nature's bounty. Two women behind the counter were measuring and bagging customers' orders. After accepting a complimentary cup of mountain tea, I retreated to the balcony to sip on sweetness and soak in the view. But it wasn't long before the sounds and smells wafting out from the room behind me enticed me back inside. I crossed over the threshold into an explosion of exotic scents.

Ioannis, the patriarch of this successful family-run business, is a combination pharmacist and medicine man. He collects thousands of herbs and spices from near and faraway places, and concocts them into teas, lotions, oils, and medicinal remedies. This particular day, he was doing his books while his wife, Crisa, measured out and bagged teas with names like *Nice Dreams* and *Brand New Day*. The sniffing and sampling of so many spices threw my senses into overload. I picked out a few favorites like Aleppo Pepper and Raz el Hanout which were carefully scooped, weighed and added to my ever-growing bag of goodies. Long after we left the village, the scent of Botano lingered in the car.

Rolf maneuvered his car around endless curves towards our next destination. The breathtaking vistas were a welcome distraction from my looming carsickness, and when we pulled into Anogia I was ready for a much-needed break.

Anogia, a large village on the north slopes of Mt. Psiloritis, shares much of the same history as many Cretan mountain villages. Occupied by the Turks and then the Germans, it has seen its share of violence and tragedy. But today it's a peaceful and welcoming town and the site of many cultural festivals and activities. The upper newer town is uninspiring, but the lower old town is quintessential Crete.

We arrived in Anogia during the busy lunch hours. Greek men gathered outside the *kafenios* drinking raki and sharing stories. *Yiayias* displayed their handiwork of intricately stitched linens. Delicious scents wafted from taverna kitchens while patrons relaxed at full tables. Handicraft shops of all kinds displayed goods on and around their doors. One of these shops was on our bucket list for the day: *Tarrha Glass Shop*.

Marios and Natassa are master crafters of hand-blown glass art. Tableware and architectural pieces, all created from glass, adorn their small workshop. When I entered the shop, my eyes fixed upon an exquisite decanter set with a unique asymmetrical look. Marios explained that he created it by hand-blowing the glass between rough stones. After admiring many other pieces of art in the shop, I left with a clear turquoise blue decanter set that reminds me of the Mediterranean waters every time I look at it.

As we departed Anogia, we became the unsuspecting victims of GPS malfunction . . . or misunderstanding. We followed all instructions by our sweet-voiced lady in a box, but arrived at a dead end on the top of a high hill.

"You have arrived at your destination."

Hardly. But it wasn't a wasted trip. To our surprise, we discovered some old World War II combat machinery at the end of the road. Rolf's and Richard's eyes lit up, and suddenly our two men were little boys again. They inspected the machinery with delight, and took turns in the rotating seat of a giant British machine gun.

After the boys had their fill of playing "war," we drove down the hill, and following signs this time, found our final destination, Zaros. This attractive little village makes its revenue by bottling and selling its clear spring waters. But Zaros' main attraction is *Lake Votamos*, a jade-green lake nestled under rocky heights about a kilometer above the village. The small lake is set within a ring of trees that shade a circular walkway, making it a charming and welcome refuge from the Cretan heat.

A lakeside taverna, *Limni*, was the perfect lunch spot to soak in the scenery and devour a meal of Cretan delicacies. We started off with simple appetizers that were artistically nestled in a basket of fresh sage and mint leaves. I leaned back into my chair, savoring the sweet moments from plate to palate, and reflected on this simple truth. *With all the unexpected surprises Crete brought into our lives, one thing remained consistent. We could always count on good food.*

On another excursion from Villa Kerasia with different friends, we climbed into Don and Sharon's VW van (the "Groovan") and took off to find a small hill village known for its local pottery. On the way, we stopped in at the organic winery of the Stinianou family, where we enjoyed a tour and a wine-tasting, compliments of the owner, Ioannis. We came away with more than a few bottles of deep red and crisp white wines as we ventured on towards our final destination: Thrapsano.

A plume of dust followed us as we wound our way along dirt roads on hot, dry hillsides. When we finally entered the pottery village, our first stop was the local taverna to tank up on fluids. After visiting a few shops, our efforts were rewarded with a stash of clay pots that we purchased for pennies on the euro. Resisting the temptation to buy more than we could carry home, we carefully loaded them into the Groovan. The entire back of the van was filled with three *pithari* (giant pots) and an array of small- to medium-sized pots. Somewhere in there, Sharon and Richard found a spot to barely squeeze in for the long trip home. (Sometimes sacrifices must be made for the important things in life.) In this case, it was authentic Greek pottery that we still enjoy mostly because of our memory of the trip. Every time I look at the pots that adorn my garden in Colorado, I smile.

I've always loved hand-thrown pottery. The whole process fascinates me and reminds me of our journey with our divine Potter. Lumps of clay in the hands of the Master evolve into a thing of absolute beauty reflective of His nature. He twists, pounds, pinches, and shapes the clay into a vessel that will hold living water. Then He puts it into the fire to strengthen and purify it. When He removes it from the fire, it looks pretty good. But He isn't finished with it yet. He wants to make this vessel into a perfect rendition of what He designed it to be. And so He sands it and washes it before gently carving and painting a one-of-a-kind design on it. Looking even better but not done yet. Back into the fire to "set" the design. Then comes the glaze. And back into the fire yet again.

"Enough!" we shout.

"Trust me," says the Potter.

You get the picture. In the end, He has created a beautiful masterpiece that He Himself, the essence of life, desires to inhabit. And interestingly, He never creates a lid. The vessel is open so that all who are drawn to its beauty can gaze into it and see the Potter reflected in its contents.

Even more beautiful than the vessel is the One who inhabits it.

BACK TO NATURE
TWO ADVENTURES

One brilliant spring morning, Richard and I made a last minute decision to join a group of other Americans from the Navy base on a day hike through the Aradena Gorge. Our spontaneity paid off and we count it as one of our top ten favorite experiences on the island.

The Aradena Gorge starts at the foot of the *Lefka Ori* (White Mountains) and descends quickly over seven kilometers ending at the Libyan Sea on the south shores of a secluded cove called Marmara Beach, accessible only by boat or on foot. We knew the hike would be considerably more difficult than other gorge hikes because of the high cliffs and boulder-filled gorge floor, but it also promised dramatic vistas and the possibility of rare flora and fauna sightings.

After crossing a wood bridge that spans the deep gorge, we began at the abandoned village of Aradena. The bridge's height makes it a popular spot for bungee jumping, but we kept our feet firmly planted on the ground and started the descent down into the gorge. The cobbled path that zigzagged down the dry mountainside was originally designed for mountain goats, donkeys, and sure-footed shepherds, so the going was slow at first. As we entered the bottom of the gorge, the trail emptied out into a canyon full of giant boulders that we had to scale to stay the course. But knowing the only way down was between the sheer rock walls, we weren't worried about getting lost.

After a 2 1/2-hour hike, the mouth of the gorge opened, revealing a glimpse of the blue waters of the Libyan Sea. We were hot and tired, and the water beckoned us to pick up the pace. All unspoken thoughts focused on how great that first plunge into the cool waters would feel. We exited the gorge onto the little beach cove, Marmara, which means marble, named for its small white beach pebbles.

Jumping into the still COLD water of the spring season was a shock to the senses. I would have probably cut my swim short, except I was curious about where our guide was taking us. He beckoned us to join him, and swam off in the direction of some caves hidden along the coastline cliffs. As I swam into the caves, I saw that they held some curious sea sculptures and captivating colors resulting from centuries of water and wind artistry. When I couldn't feel my feet anymore and my teeth were chattering, I returned to the beach and soaked up the warmth from the pebbles under me and the sun above me.

After our swim and enough rest, we continued up to a path that hugged the slope high above the sea. The view was astonishing. I reminded myself to keep my eyes on the path. One misstep would have sent me tumbling down into the water, and I'd had my swim already.

We hiked past the still visible ruins of ancient *Finix (or Phoenix)*, a major city and port during Roman and Byzantine times. Many ships wintered in this natural sheltered port to escape from the brutal winds and storms of the season. In fact, the ship that carried Apostle Paul en route to Rome headed for this harbor but encountered bad weather that drove it farther out to sea (Acts 27:9–26.) Below ancient Finix and nestled into a spacious natural harbor is the modern town of Loutro, a seaside village accessible only by boat or on foot. In the off-season, Loutro is a sleepy little town of roughly a dozen inhabitants who enjoy the quiet as they prepare the town for the flush of summer tourism. We descended upon the only taverna that was open for a well-needed, well-deserved lunch, washed down with a cold beer. Sitting at the water's edge gazing over the clear smooth sea, we chatted about the hike, the food, and the incredible sight before us.

As we basked in the early spring sunshine and the warm conversation between hiking-companions-turned-friends, my thoughts turned to those of curious expectation. *What other adventures await us on this diverse and wild island that we now call home?* I wished the day would never end and pondered on how we could extend our next outdoor adventure.

And then it hit me. Long days of exploring without cars or crowds, and quiet nights where the floor is sand and the ceiling is star-filled sky.

Camping.

Crete has very few organized campsites. Unfortunately, many pristine areas have been ruined by filthy humans who have no respect for the land. Anyone intending on camping "off trail" must tread lightly and remember, "If you pack it in, you pack it out." And also, be aware of private property boundaries; otherwise, you may end up with a Cretan knife under your nose in the morning (just kidding . . . sort of . . .).

"Bring me your gear and we'll stuff it all in here."

We were standing in our driveway with our friends, Cameron and Shelby, looking skeptical at Shelby's attempts to shove our camping items, including two coolers, into our small Honda sedan.

How are we all going to fit in here with everything? I thought.

Shelby and Cameron were our go-to, hang-out, come-on-over, like-family best friends. No matter that they were half our age, we jokingly called each other, "the kids." In any case, fun bubbled up when we put our heads together, and today we had camping in our sights. But first we had to pack the car.

"Shelby, this is NOT all going to fit in that little car!" I said.

"Sure it will, Just watch. You can put the cooler under your feet and I'll sit in back on top of the tent. Cameron will hold the bags in his lap."

Richard suppressed a chuckle. He knew he was safe from any contortionist seating arrangements because he was the driver. Cameron and I weren't so sure. But Shelby wasn't deterred. Most of the creative energy from our group flowed from her inventive mind. She would get an idea in her head, sell it to Cameron, who was more than willing to indulge her, and together they would dress it up and present it to us in such a way that we couldn't resist. They could make a root canal sound fun.

Miraculously, we managed to squeeze everything (and everyone) into our car with a minimal amount of discomfort. Richard drove southwest towards our destination on the south coast, where we left our car in Sougia and hit the trail to ancient Lissos. This 4-kilometer trail was once used by pilgrims seeking the healing waters in the *Asklepion*, (temple of healing) built against the cliffs next to a curative spring.

The first part of the hike was pleasant as we passed under the shade of oleander and tamarisk trees. Soon, we arrived at a dramatic gorge with towering stone cliffs where the path ascended to a high plateau that was much warmer and very dry.

As we tramped up the steep section of the trail, I heard Shelby behind me, laughing out loud.

"What's so funny?" I asked.

"Your pack is almost bigger than you, and I just saw an image of you falling over on your back like a stranded turtle," she giggled, motioning to my green windbreaker.

I was too exhausted to enjoy the joke, but the nickname stuck and I was henceforth referred to as "Turtle."

The trail traversed across the flat plateau, winding its way through thorny undergrowth and dry sagebrush, intersecting a few small trees like a dot-to-dot puzzle. At the end of the plateau, the view opened up to the vast Libyan Sea and the secluded Lissos cove far below us. The sudden descent into Lissos ended at the welcome shade of a grove of trees where a well-marked spring gushed out pure cold water. We filled our water bottles at this lush oasis before continuing down to the seaside.

Once we set up camp under the trees near the cove, we soaked in the quiet beauty of this ancient place. In Hellenistic and Roman times, Lissos flourished as the harbor city of Elyros, until the Saracens destroyed it in the ninth century. Roman chamber tombs, threshing floors, and ancient walls dotted the hillside. Historians say at its peak the area of Lissos was home to over 30,000 inhabitants. The Lissos coins with the image of the goddess Artemis on one side and a dolphin on the reverse were among the artifacts excavated from this area . The number of statues discovered in Lissos is second only to Gortys, the Roman capital city of Crete.

Modern-day excavations recently revealed a well-preserved mosaic floor and the remains of a theater, aqueducts, Roman baths, and buildings. Two miniscule chapels embellished with age-faded Byzantine frescoes and recycled Roman marble blocks stand silent among the trees. Because Lissos was an important sacred healing center, archeologists expect many more treasures are hidden under the Cretan landscape that is now home to ancient olive trees, herds of goats, and the occasional wanderer.

And wander we did. Hiking the hills around Lissos was a scavenger hunt with surprises around every tree. Discovering a huge threshing floor high above our campsite made us realize the sheer size of the original settlement.

Sitting on one of the old stones that encircled the ancient threshing floor, I imagined what life was like so many centuries ago. People worked, played, worshipped, married, raised families, and died with the same gamut of emotions we feel today. From elated joy to deep despair, we have the human condition in common throughout the ages. I wondered how many before us had enjoyed friendship and fellowship around a fire on the pebble beach.

As the day came to a close, these twenty-first-century wanderers relaxed by the campfire and toasted our friendship with cool wine and roasted marshmallows. The darkness settled in and a brilliant canopy of stars filled the night sky. And then, just when we thought it couldn't get any better, a full moon rose over the black water.

HEADING WEST
THE LAST FRONTIER

The Gramvousa peninsula and its eastern cousin Roudopou peninsula cradle the beautiful Bay of Kissamos between them. Gramvousa itself is a smaller spit of land compared to the Roudopou, but boasts many scenic spots to enjoy the Mediterranean day and nightlife. We discovered this area of northwest Crete on our bicycles one early spring weekend.

West of the Kissamos port, the landscape turns very rural. The highway changes into a narrow two-lane road that veers south to the other side of the island. The only road that accesses the Gramvousa Peninsula is a rough dirt road leading north to the tip and to some spectacular views. It's a slow, bumpy drive over washed-out, crumbling roadbeds with no services, only a variety of goats and sheep grazing along the road, some of whom are tame and curious; others are just plain annoying.

We parked our car at the foot of the Gramvousa road and grabbed a quick picnic snack. It wasn't long before one goat, a particularly bold fellow, became very interested in relieving Richard of his bag of potato chips. He made a complete nuisance of himself, even going so far as to butt a few chips out of Richard's hand. When we finally mounted our bikes, I completely expected him to trot along beside us, but he seemed to understand that we didn't take the chips with us and instead, snorted at our departure.

We biked northward on the ascending jeep trail that rose along the protected east side of the peninsula. After ten kilometers, we arrived at a rough gravel parking lot where a seasonal taverna was abandoned on this early spring day, closed and boarded up against the winter winds. We ditched our bikes and hiked over the ridge to see the west side of the peninsula. As soon as we crested the hill, the west winds nearly blasted us off our feet but what took our breath away was the view. From this vantage point, we saw the expansive view west that includes Gramvousa Island off the tip of Crete, and directly below us, picturesque Balos Bay, a postcard-famous beach. Variegated shades of blues and greens gave dimension to the clear water, and the empty sand beach seemed to beckon us to come down for a swim. A well-trodden rock stair path led downwards, tempting us to follow it to Balos, but the wind finally drove us back to the secluded side of the peninsula. We vowed to return when warmer weather arrived.

And return we did. Later that summer, a group of us joined the crowds of tourists on a ferry bound for Balos. Our first stop out from Kissamos port was Gramvousa Island, the site of a very important Venetian fortress that held out against the Turks long after mainland Crete fell. We lathered up with sunscreen and donned our hats for the short but hot hike up to the fortress ruins. From the walls of the long abandoned fortress the views over the bay south to the mainland were spectacular. By the time we made it back to the boat, we were overheated and dripping with sweat, so we were ecstatic to see that the crew had rigged a long slide from the second deck. They encouraged us to experience a jaw-dropping plunge into the clear, cool waters below, and we were more than happy to oblige.

Afterwards, the ferry motored us to Balos Bay and dropped anchor in the shallows. The passengers spilled out and made a beeline to the shore to claim a spot for the afternoon. They dispersed along the huge beach, hurriedly dropping beach supplies and erecting umbrellas before finding refuge from the sweltering heat in the shallow, refreshing water. We joined them in the hot pursuit of cool water and laying on our back in the shallows, we marveled at this place of natural beauty and pristine surroundings.

A few kilometers from Balos lay another popular beachcombing destination. Pressing westward, we set our sights on Falassarna. Big beaches + ancient ruins + kite sailing + rustic hotels + good food - crowds = Falassarna. It's easy to see why this huge beach is a favorite among the locals. Because of its remote location, it lacks the crowds of tourists that opt for closer beach spots along the north shore near Hania.

Falassarna used to be nothing more than a deserted expansive beach with no facilities. In recent years, a few tavernas and small hotels moved in to accommodate the few visitors that were attracted by its simplicity and ruggedness. Falassarna is a peaceful and mesmeric place with not much else to do but walk, swim, and take in the beautiful surroundings. Many locals flock there to escape the city heat and tourists in the summer. In the winter, it's a favorite spot for kite sailing and windsurfing. In all seasons, it has a reputation for brutal west winds that howl over the sea and stir up the sand dunes. But it is the perfect spot to view a Mediterranean sunset.

Whenever we got the itch to head west to Falassarna, we first tried to second guess if the wind was kicking up there. The weather in Hania was no indicator of the weather on the far west coast. Hania could be completely calm, but just 60 kilometers west, Falassarna could be engulfed in a howling tempest. One such day we forged ahead with the idea of Plan B in the back of our minds (seek shelter in a local taverna and eat and drink and play card games for the next three hours while watching the surf kick up and the sand swirl).

Much to our surprise, we made our way down to the beach area without being blown off our feet. In fact, Big Beach was almost empty, so we happily paid the €6 fee for a couple of chairs and settled in under the shade of the umbrella that barely moved in the light breeze. After a swim in the chilly water and a picnic lunch, we walked over to the ancient ruins of Falassarna that were being excavated.

Falassarna was an ancient port, the site of a dominant Hellenistic navy that flourished in the third and fourth centuries. Now its ruins include city walls, houses, tombs, and a curious stone throne that perhaps was erected in honor of Poseidon, the god of the sea. But the most puzzling aspect of the port was its location on a rise above the coast instead of at the water's edge. In AD 365, an earthquake of unprecedented proportions heaved the west coast of Crete up 6–9 meters, causing major geographical changes. The elevated port was useless, and the surrounding settlement was eventually abandoned. Falassarna submitted once again to Mother Nature.

As we gazed out over the western horizon and watched the glimmering sun melt into the sea, it was hard to believe that this place was once a hub of activity. We were sitting in a quiet taverna perched on the hill above the main beach. The vibrant reds and oranges of the sunset infused every droplet of condensation on our stubby wine glasses. The day came to a close over this vision of serenity and beauty, and the air was unusually still. For today, the winds of Falassarna were silent.

EASTER ON THE ISLAND
ΚΑΛΟ ΠΑΣΧΑ (HAPPY EASTER)

One April morning we ventured into the picturesque seaside town of Kissamos-Kastelli, on the far northwest end of Crete. The much anticipated celebration of *Carnivali,* or Greek Mardi Gras, that kicks off the Easter Lenten season was in full swing. Each city in Greece has their own version of *Carnivali,* an elaborate and sometimes chaotic parade of masqueraders that typically outnumber the spectators.

Kissamos-Kastelli vibrated with anticipation that Sunday morning in April. We sat along the parade route on a low wall near the central park, a couple of conspicuous foreigners amidst hundreds of older Greeks. A tiny toddler outfitted in a hot pink tutu and a glittering tiara was the only splash of color in a sea of black-clad geriatric spectators.

Where were all the young people? we wondered. It didn't take us long to find out. Most of them were in the parade that was finally inching its way towards us after a delayed "island time" start. This small town overflowed beyond its 2,000 inhabitants, most of whom were active participants in the Carnivali parade.

No Macy's Day parade, this was a bewildering conglomeration of costumes, floats, and noise. The flatbed trailer floats strained under the weight of whistle blowing, brightly costumed participants reveling in their moment of glory. The design of the floats ranged anywhere from the elaborate to the last-minute throw-something-together–in-my-back-yard-because-I-want-to-be-in-the-parade float. Occasionally, we detected a theme but that was usually a stretch. But what they lacked in design, they compensated for in exuberance. Every participant was suddenly transformed into a happy-go-lucky child, doing their best to draw anyone and everyone in the crowd into their celebration. Conspicuously absent were the marching bands of typical American parades. Instead, a loud speaker blared frantic nightclub music and parade participants gyrated to the rhythm. Above the noise, the master of ceremonies shouted in rapid-fire Greek.

In direct contrast to this chaotic display of gaiety were the Cretan dancers. Maintaining stoic expressions and impeccable order, they gracefully walked, hands on hips, displaying the distinguishable costumes of their particular region of Crete. Some floats were political in nature, but most were just playful. An impressive castle of enormous dimensions rolled by, complete with royal princes and princesses, prompting oohs and ahhs from the crowd.

But the next float that came into view roused catcalls and laughter from the crowd. A flatbed trailer decked out in pink paper and tacky flowers rolled down the street. On it, a dozen or more half-dressed grown men in long blonde wigs danced and primped to the Barbie theme. Pathetic . . . but funny.

My personal favorite was the group that brought up the rear. Over a hundred pita souvlakis of every size, shape, and age danced down the street. A high collar of foam french fries, lettuce, tomatoes, and shaved lamb protruded from the pita that wrapped snug around their bodies. And on top of their barely visible heads was a dollop of tzatziki sauce that looked like a strange beret. Where else but Greece could you see such a spectacle?! The littlest "pita" was a chap about 3 years old—so cute I could've eaten him. If the pita parade was an attempt to roust up business for the local cafés, it worked. Everyone's thoughts turned to food, and not long after the parade, they filled the tavernas to capacity.

Carnivali confirmed my observations about the Greek people. Despite the harsh economic crisis that affected every household on Crete, most Greeks readily participated in any kind of revelry, and turned the simplest of affairs into a memorable event. I learned that detailed planning isn't always necessary to throw a successful party. In fact, the more spontaneous, the better. I began to appreciate the laid-back island vibe that has no need for scheduling and over-planning. Many times we were surprised and delighted by friends dropping in. And it wasn't unusual for invitations to dinner, coffee or a side trip to come as a quick phone call or text on the same day.

"Let's grab a coffee. I'll meet you at *Koukouvia*." An hour later, Marina and I sat at a table in a café perched high above the harbor of Hania. Admiring the view and sipping on our cappuccinos, the conversation turned towards the upcoming Easter season.

"How do you celebrate Easter here on Crete?" I asked her.

"We call Easter *Pascha,* meaning Passover, and it's the most important religious holiday in Greece. The preparations during Holy Week lead up to the big event of Resurrection Sunday. Remember when you and Richard went to Stavros Cove on Clean Monday? That was the start of the Lenten season."

Only a few days earlier, on Clean Monday, Richard and I participated in the traditional Greek festivities marking the end of the *Carnavali* revelry, and the beginning of the 40-day Lenten fast. Clean Monday also marks the first day of spring, so it wasn't surprising to see the entire town outdoors setting up picnics and flying kites. The day was festive as locals packed the little square at Stavros Cove. Live musicians entertained the crowd with traditional Greek music, and spectators of all ages circled up in a spontaneous Greek dance.

As is the custom with every Greek gathering, the tables groaned under copious amounts of food. Elaborate seafood and shellfish dishes included octopus, cuttlefish, shrimp, and mussels. Meat, dairy, and eggs forbidden during Lent, were conspicuously absent. But the sheer volume and variety of the side dishes that accompanied the seafood was plentiful. Plates of stuffed grape leaves (*domades*), giant beans (*gigantes*) and a variety of salads accompanied baskets of flat breads called *laganas* and small bowls of wrinkled Cretan olives. All delicious. But a pink dip that looked deceivingly like a sweet gelatinous fruit concoction was a bewildering shock to the taste buds. My first big bite of *taramosalata,* fish roe dip was my last.

Besides consuming large amounts of fasting food, Clean Monday tradition calls for a vast display of kite flying. During the previous week, I picked out our own blue and white kite (the colors of the Greek flag) from over a hundred kites of different shapes and sizes in our small village market. We joined the festivities on the beach as dozens of people coaxed their kites up and away. In no time, the sky fluttered with colorful kites like captive birds that danced and swayed on the sea breeze.

Marina reminded me that every Greek Orthodox family holds tradition close as they prepare for Holy Week leading up to Resurrection Sunday. Families attend daily church services and observe seasonal traditions in the home:

Holy Tuesday – The women bake *Koulourakia,* a butter cookie, golden in color and rich with flavors of vanilla and orange.

Holy Wednesday – Members of local orthodox churches receive Holy Unction (anointing of holy oil) as a remembrance of the prostitute who anointed Christ's head and feet with costly oil to the dismay of the disciples during the week before his crucifixion (Matthew 26:6–13).

Holy Thursday – Women and children dye hard-boiled eggs a deep red, representing the blood of Christ shed on the cross. These eggs (which represent the closed tomb of Christ) are nestled into a braided traditional Easter bread called *tsoureki.* In the evening, the churches hold the very lengthy Holy Passion service where the twelve lessons of the Gospels are read.

Good Friday – A day of mourning recognizing the crucifixion of Christ. The faithful follow strict protocol in their devotion, including abstaining from sweets. During the day, the women and girls meet at the local church and meticulously decorate the funeral bier (*Epitaphios* of Christ) with fresh flowers and embroidered cloths. Many stores sell ornate candles to take to the evening service.

The Good Friday evening vesper service ends with a solemn procession of the *Epitaphios*. This event radiates simple beauty and deep symbolism. Cantors, clergy, and faithful congregants carry candles and sing mournful chants as they follow the bier. Long lines of moving candles and sad intonations fill the night as the procession moves through the village.

As Marina and I finished our coffee and conversation, she turned to me and offered an invitation.

"Why don't you join me on Holy Saturday for the Easter Mass? It will be at *Chrysopigi Monastery* in Hania. Such a beautiful setting, Mel. You must come!"

I was thrilled to be invited to this sacred service and I counted the days until Saturday.

Dusk was falling when Marina and I arrived at the monastery. We entered through its thick wooden doors into a large stone courtyard filled with the fragrance of blooming orange trees. The church was already filled to capacity, so we sat among the mostly silent crowd that had gathered in the courtyard. All was in darkness. I managed to inch my way to the doors of the church and watched in wonder as the service began. The chapel was silent as the priest began to read from the Holy Scriptures. The sound of incantations, the sight of dimmed lighting and the smell of incense gave me goose bumps. But what happened next left me awestruck.

At midnight, the most significant event of the year began. All lights were extinguished, plunging the church into complete darkness and silence. The priest emerged from behind the curtain at the altar carrying a single candle lit from the holy flame brought from Jerusalem. He walked to the nuns who were at the front of the church and lit their candles. As the flame passed from person to person, the cold darkness of the church succumbed to the glimmering warmth of light. The nuns began singing a song that translated, "Jesus Christ has risen from the dead." They moved down the center aisle followed by the congregants. Everyone exited into the darkened courtyard where more people waited to receive the light.

Even more beautiful than the sight of hundreds of candles in the silence was the knowledge that all of Greece was taking part in this same holy moment, the receiving of the light of the resurrection honored for hundreds of years in the church's history. The pristine little courtyard filled with blazing candlelight under the large orange trees fragrant with their blossoms. Solemn faces changed to smiles, handshakes and kisses. The greeting, "*Christos Anesti!*" (Christ is Risen!) followed by "*Alithos Anesti!*" (Indeed He has Risen!) echoed through the crowd, and Marina and I joined them. Everyone dispersed to their cars, carefully ensuring that their candle remained lit until they got home. Upon arriving at their threshold, they marked a sooty cross above their doorway to ensure blessing on the home and good luck in the coming year.

And then the celebration began in earnest.

The aftermath of midnight mass and the breaking of the fast was a jubilation equivalent to a pyromaniacs' dream. After leaving Marina around 1:00 in the morning, I headed home. As I rounded a corner, I stopped cold in the middle of the road. Before me, an effigy of Judas stood ablaze on the summit of a giant bonfire. Shouts of laughter and fireworks filled the air. Church bells pierced the night. Houses were brightly lit and the aroma of slow-roasted lamb on the spit wafted from nearly every front terrace. The tables were laden with food—Easter breads and cookies, rice pilafi, various salads and drinks like wine and raki. Children ran around with their red Easter eggs engaging each other in the egg cracking game called *tsougrisma*. (Representing the breaking open of the tomb.) Feasting, fireworks and live music continued throughout the night and into the early morning hours.

I felt refreshed by the deep spiritual observation of Holy Week in Crete, (the Easter Bunny was not a participant) and I knew that I would never look at Easter the same way again. The devotion and strict adherence to ritual and tradition are criticized by some as unnecessary, but I disagree. If anything, the observance of Holy Week with its extravagant preparation, deep solemnity, and jubilant celebration only deepens the reality of the most significant event in Christian history.

SUMMER

After a sleepy winter and spring, we noticed that the island began waking up right before Easter. The locals busied themselves with a cleanup campaign that impressed even the Germans here. Potholes filled, roads repaired, construction sites hummed, hardware stores crowded, terraces and pathways scrubbed, and walls (and tree trunks) given a new coat of whitewash. What began as a symbolic washing to prepare for Lent continued throughout the spring, and the island buzzed as it prepared for the annual arrival of its most welcome guests: summer and the tourists.

Spring on Crete is like a gentle simmering of expectation; a pot of goodness warming up on the stove, slowly infusing all the flavors together. Turn up the heat and you get a full rolling boil of goodness exploding with flavor. This is Crete in the summer. It pulsates with life. Everything and everyone moves outdoors. Taverna tables spill out into the cobbled streets, patios gush with blooming herbs and flowers, and people linger on street corners and terraces relishing in the cool night air, a respite from the day's heat. During that heat, the beaches swell with the sights and sounds of summer. Umbrellas stretch along the seashore, their tips touching in a parade of color, and a symphony of beach sounds echo over the warm waters—the laughter of children playing in the sea, the popping of paddleboard balls, the clinking of beer bottles in a nearby taverna. And everywhere, the low murmurs of several foreign languages float on the air.

Summer exhales hot days and clear skies over tranquil and refreshing seawater. Nights pulsate with the scent of jasmine intermingled with far away music. They dance together on the breeze as if celebrating of the coolness of the evening.

Summer is also energized by two major groups of people: Tourists and the people who serve them. This island of 600,000 inhabitants swells to over 2 million during the summer months, but Crete welcomes them with warm hospitality. From the popular beach hangouts to the remote mountain villages, the Greeks consistently practice *xenia*, the art of courtesy and generosity shown to a stranger or foreigner.

Agriculture and tourism are the driving forces behind Crete's economy, and in the summertime the two collide with gusto. Full red tomatoes exploding with flavor and ripe watermelons gushing with sweet juice are only two of the Cretan delicacies that grace the dining tables around the island. The *laikis* (farmers' markets) boast an array of colorful and pungent produce, honey, olive oil, and seafood.

Summer is grilled veggies and fresh fruit from the morning laiki, beach picnics with friends, the heady fragrance of wild thyme and jasmine, cloudless skies over the Akrotiri, evening swims as the sun melts into the sea, full moon viewing over Marathi Beach, and the daily no-brainer wardrobe of a pair of sandals and a sundress.

Summer is blue and white, the colors of the Greek flag. Blue skies, blue water, white sands, white heat.

I'm sitting on the back shaded terrace relishing the cool breeze from the sea. These early summer mornings are wonderfully peaceful. The temps hover around 70, and the breeze from the sea is so soothing. I try to take full advantage of it by walking, working, or reading outside, because I know it won't be long before the oppressive heat of summer hits, when the only comfort found is in the refuge of an air-conditioned room or the cool sea water. But for now, it's 7:00 a.m., and I'm sitting on our back terrace, listening to the sounds of the countryside waking up—the birds, the sheep, the roosters, and a few cars in the distance. A fresh beach towel hanging on the clothesline above me flaps in the breeze. In a few hours, all those sounds will be drowned out by the chaotic hum of the cicadas (those noisy little sun-worshipers) in the olive trees. They signal the beginning of summer, and the hotter it gets, the louder they sing.

BEATING THE HEAT IN CRETE
ROAD TRIP TO PALEOCHORA

Summer (*kalokeri*) arrived on the heels of strong springtime sirocco winds, big, blustery winds that stir up the red "Kadhafi dust" from Libya and make you want to put a gun to your head. As a resident of the island once remarked:

> *Came spring, and Africa had its voice in our affairs: 'the Big Tongue' as the old women of Crete call the hot, dust-laden sorokos that comes howling up from Libya. The first day of a sorokos was bad enough; the second was even worse; and by the third you were ready to commit murder or suicide. The air became clogged with yellow dust, you felt restless and often had a headache, couldn't work, couldn't read, couldn't do anything. Tempers wore thin, quarrels flared, domestic peace was threatened. But the essence of the Cretan climate is the imminence of sudden change; and so the south wind would leave as quickly as it had come, and then for a few days peace and calm seas and blue skies were ours. But never for long -always another wind would come,*

and some of them, like the cool meltemia breezes that blew
steadily from the northwest for forty days in summer, were
most welcome."

—*Winds of Crete*, by David MacNeil Doren, 1974

As summer rolled in so did the hot temperatures averaging around 30C (90F) with nights in the high 70s and 80s. Thankfully, the humidity was only around 40–50 percent, so it was ideal. But where is the best place to beat the heat? Anywhere around or even better, IN the water. The beautiful, azure, clear, warm, deep, gentle, inviting water of the Aegean Sea. And on an island, there's never a lack of this coastal pleasure.

Many of the out-of-the-way havens for fun, food and nightlife lie on the south coast of Crete. One of these hidden treasures fast became our favorite: *Paleochora*, a small beach town with an enjoyable end of the road, laid-back feel. Paleochora, originally known as Kastel Selinou, is located on a spit of land about six blocks wide that juts out into the Libyan Sea. The compact little town center sits below the ruins of an old fortress built by the Venetians in 1279. In 1539, the famous pirate, Barbarossa, destroyed the fortress. Never restored, its low ancient walls provide the perfect perch for a stellar view down to the harbor and over the Libyan Sea.

On our first excursion to Paleochora, we drove over the mountain range and arrived in town by early afternoon. To our delight, we discovered Paleochora was smaller and lacked the glitz of many resort towns on the north coast. A sandy beach defined the west side of the spit, and the east side boasted a warm pebble beach. Depending on the direction of the wind, you could always find a quiet beach spot on the opposite side of town. We opted to park our beach towels on the pebble side and enjoyed an afternoon swim.

It wasn't long before hunger drove us off the beach and in search of food. Walking along the small streets lined with homes and businesses, we discovered a small art studio just a block off the main street. As we entered the shop, a woman with gleaming black hair and huge blue eyes greeted us. Her name was Manto, and we soon discovered that her classic beauty was second only to her creative talent. She was a Greek artist with an eye for detail and a heart for hospitality.

"*Kalimera*! How are you today?" she asked with a smile.

"Very well, thank you! What a beautiful shop you have here. Do you do all the painting?"

"Yes, I take most of my inspiration from the gardens around Crete."

Her artwork, each depicting a simple Mediterranean scene in dramatic color, filled every inch of wall space, proving she was not only talented but prolific as well. Pomegranates, lemons, and flowers shared the space with grapes, olive branches and Minoan princesses. A variety of canvases hung from the wall, from a simple, single oleander blossom on a 4″ square wood plaque to a splash of grapes on an antique wine barrel stave.

We lingered for a long time, admiring her art and engaging in lively conversation. It became obvious that Manto was a hardworking, savvy businesswoman with a passion for sharing Greek hospitality.

"I converted this old house into a studio for me and rooms for rent upstairs. Would you like to see the rooms?"

Ignoring our hunger pangs, we jumped at the chance to spend more time in her company and learn about the culture of Paleochora through the eyes of a local. She opened the door of one of the rooms and light bounced off the murals and paintings that graced the white walls. The space was immaculate, modern, and decorated with her own signature style. A more sophisticated creation on large canvas adorned the wall above the bed.

"Oh, how lovely!" I exclaimed. "You don't happen to have a vacancy for a couple of nights, do you?"

She laughed, "This room here is for you."

With a handshake and a hug, we left her to lock up for afternoon siesta and we went off in search of a late lunch.

That night, we slept soundly in a quiet room filled with Manto's touch of artistry. And after sleeping both nights under a wild Cretan garden, I knew I had to take it home with me. Today, the large canvas hangs above my bed in my Colorado home.

One treasure often leads to another.

"You must go to *To Skolio* for lunch," said Manto. We sat at a table together in her café, sharing stories over a cup of espresso and an ample breakfast from the buffet. (She and her husband transformed an old space next to her studio into a top-rated breakfast place.)

Our ears immediately perked at the sound of advice from a local.

"The café is up a small gorge not too far from here. About five kilometers up the gorge is a town called Anidri. It is very tiny but the old schoolhouse (*skolio*) is converted into a taverna. You MUST go," she emphasized.

That afternoon, we walked into a bike shop in town. A Greek gentleman greeted us and balked at our request to rent bikes to ride up the Anidri Gorge.

"No, you cannot ride bicycles in the gorge."

"Why not?" we inquired, thinking he meant we weren't allowed to take his bicycles that far out of town.

"It is very . . . up." He gave me the full up-and-down look. "Your husband maybe make it, but not you."

He did his best to dissuade us, but we persisted and he reluctantly gave in with a backhanded remark.

"OK, but first we fit bike for your husband," he said with an arrogant tip of his dark head. "You're in Greece now. Men are first." I knew for a fact that wasn't true since I had experienced only the deepest respect from Greek men towards women. They were especially fond of (or afraid of) their mothers. I remembered the line from the movie, *My Big Fat Greek Wedding*, "The man may be the head of the family, but the woman is the neck that turns the head." I reasoned that this man had a real pain-in-the-neck mother. Either way, I grew impatient with his condescending attitude and couldn't get away from him quick enough. He rented us two substandard bikes and we forged on, anticipating our adventure while making a mental note to bring our own bikes next time.

Outside of town, we ascended up the narrow road into a gorge cut by a creek reduced to a summer trickle. Passing olive groves, goat herds, and dilapidated sheds, we peddled up to our destination and arrived in better shape than I expected, ready for a good meal and a cold beer.

To Skolio taverna is an old restored schoolhouse with a patio in the back shaded by an enormous olive tree. The tables and chairs wobbled on the uneven stone terrace, and a few cats freely roamed the area looking for handouts. What set this eatery apart was not only the interesting Greek/French/international cuisine but also the stunning view from high above the Libyan Sea.

After lunch, the ride down the gorge was fast and exhilarating. At the bottom of the gorge we turned hard left and peddled out the dusty hot road along the shore towards a beach that quickly became our favorite spot. Gialskari Beach was once a hot camping spot for vagabonds and hippies in the 70s, and still today holds onto a little of that flavor. But it grew up very gracefully compared to many other resort beaches that succumbed to massive changes born out of the tourism boom. Gialskari has nothing to boast about except that your ordinary needs will be met in an extraordinary setting.

One of my husband's requirements of a beach is that it must have some shade. How a man who doesn't like sun, sand, or the water ended up on a Mediterranean island is beyond me. Except to say, he learned quickly to come out of his comfort zone. Lucky for him, and me, Gialskari hit every button for us about what makes a great beach. Instead of sand, the beach consisted of small round pebbles that soaked up the sun's warmth, and the tamarisk trees provided full shade. We rented a couple of lounge chairs, set up camp under the trees, and grabbed our snorkel gear.

After hours in the water, the wind and the surf began to pick up so we sought refuge at a cove we saw in the distance. As we approached the cove, the waves thrashed around us and finally spit us up onto the beach. Removing our sand-covered masks, we looked up and realized we were being observed by a crowd of people – completely naked people. No tan lines here. We sheepishly smiled and waved, and discreetly turned our backs on them pretending to gaze out over the waves while in reality planning our escape. But the sun and silence was so welcoming that we lingered longer than we intended, and it was with some regret that we slid back into the sea and set our sights for our own beach spot.

We were famished by the time we returned to our beach towels on Gialskari, and so we retired to the single outdoor taverna under the trees. Gobbling down a Greek salad, some calamari, and a couple of cold beers, we laughed hysterically over our nudie beach crashing experience.

"You should have seen your face!"

"No, you should have seen YOURS!"

While we never completely shed our prudish American modesty, we learned to accept that most Mediterranean beaches have an unofficial "nudie section." Northern Europeans rather than local Greeks usually populate these pockets of liberation. Understandable. Most of them left the frigid miserable weather of Germany or Denmark to bask in the warm sun and sand of Crete - naked.

What could make Gialskari Beach more perfect, you say? A spa? They had that, too. Around the corner from the taverna, a chalkboard sign listing the day's specials was propped outside a tiny grass hut under the trees. Massage, haircut, pedicure, reflexology—a lot of magic in a little space. A young entrepreneurial German expat had opened the shop many years ago, and if the APPOINTMENTS RECOMMENDED sign was any indication, I'd say she has a good thing going.

After a full day in the sun, we fought the temptation to flop into bed early, opting instead to join in the fun of Paleochora's summer nightlife. The main street closed down to traffic and the area transformed into an outdoor party. Tables, chairs, and music spilled out from the tavernas into the street where old men played backgammon, young tourists drank raki, and everyone relished in the activity.

Including us.

What's the perfect ending to a perfect Cretan beach day? A scoop of lemon gelato, a warm summer breeze off the sea, and a table for two in the middle of the night action. We were in love with Paleochora.

But just when we thought it couldn't get better, another south coast gem wooed us to its shores.

LOVE IN LOUTRO

A GREEK BEAUTY

Imagine the idyllic Greek location. I see blue-shuttered white buildings hugging the shoreline of a large secluded cove. Small fishing boats sway as they strain against the ropes that tether them to the docks. And the whole peaceful scene is reflected in the clear, deep Mediterranean waters. This is Loutro, a tiny seaside town set beneath the high, arid hills of Sfakia on the south coast.

Historically, it was once an important port town in Hellenistic and Roman times when it was known as Phoenix. Many sailing vessels were frequent visitors to this natural harbor. In AD 90, St. Paul was a prisoner on a ship bound for Rome when one of his companions recorded their voyage along the south coast of Crete.

Much time had been lost, and sailing had already become dangerous because by now it was after the Day of Atonement. So Paul warned them, "Men, I can see that our voyage is going to be disastrous and bring great loss to ship and cargo, and to our own lives also." But the centurion, instead of listening to what Paul said, followed the advice of

the pilot and of the owner of the ship. Since the harbor was
unsuitable to winter in, the majority decided that we should
sail on, hoping to reach Phoenix and winter there. This was
a harbor in Crete, facing both southwest and northwest.
When a gentle south wind began to blow, they saw their
opportunity; so they weighed anchor and sailed along the
shore of Crete. Before very long, a wind of hurricane force,
called the Northeaster, swept down from the island. The
ship was caught by the storm and could not head into the
wind; so we gave way to it and were driven along.

(Recorded by Luke in Acts 27:9–15)

Spoiler alert: Not so happy ending. They ended up shipwrecked
on the island of Malta.

In the winter months, Loutro completely closes down. The
local population during that time is roughly eight people and
about twice as many cats. In the summer months, this miniature
waterfront explodes with laid back sun worshippers, 95 percent
of whom are visitors. But somehow it still manages to preserve the
small village feel. You won't find discos, loud parties, cars, buses,
or scooters. You *will* find a peaceful, relaxing, stunningly beautiful
place to get away from it all. Perhaps it's the signature white-
and-blue painted buildings or the fact that it is only accessible
by boat or on foot. Either way, it is a favorite destination for
locals and tourists alike. If you're looking for high adventure or
buzzing nightlife, go elsewhere. This little town's claim to fame is
its location on a expansive blue cove where the water is so clear

and the village so welcoming it's hard to leave its secluded shores at the end of the day.

On a hot day in June we boarded the 1:00 ferry in Hora Sfakia, anticipating an afternoon of relaxation under an umbrella on the pebble beach of Loutro. A few passengers lined the rail of the ferry as it chugged along the rugged south coast. Forty-five minutes later we pulled into the cement dock of Loutro and walked towards the pebble beach. *Let the magic begin*, I thought to myself.

There is really nothing to do in Loutro. And that's the magic of it. No frantic water sports, no nightclubs, and no noise. A few tiny homes and small hotels inch up the hillside, but for the most part, Loutro's few businesses all coexist side by side along the water's edge.

We set our towels on two beach chairs inches away from the water's edge, donned our snorkel gear, and paddled out into the cove on a rented kayak. For the next two hours, we explored the cracks and crevices along the rocky coast of the cove. Bright orange and red starfish gripped the sides of their underwater ledges and schools of tiny fish swarmed around us. The sea water was so buoyant that we never tired while snorkeling, and the time flew by. Well past 4:00, we made our way back to shore and air-dried in the late afternoon sun on the warm pebble beach.

Afterwards, we leisurely poked around in the little tourist shops, ate the morning's catch seafood at one of the waterside tavernas, and engaged in a lively conversation with a giant caged parrot outside one of the small hotels. Did I say there's nothing to do in Loutro? We somehow managed to keep ourselves so busy that the loud mournful blow of the approaching ferry's horn came as a complete surprise. Looking at a nearby clock, we realized the 6:00 p.m. ferry was right on time to pick up day-trippers, including us, and ferry them back to Hora Sfakia. We made our reluctant exit, vowing to return and stay longer.

And we did. Sooner than expected.

In August of that same summer, we experienced Loutro's magic again. One of the items on my bucket list was to attend a Greek wedding. And this was not just any Greek wedding. This was the daughter of our dear friends, Nick and Marina. Richard and I felt honored to be invited, and I felt doubly blessed when they asked me to sing during the ceremony. This was a wedding mixed with Greek Orthodox and Western traditions, since the bride and groom hailed from different cultures.

The idyllic Mediterranean beauty of Loutro makes it a popular choice for weddings. On this particular occasion, the presence of good friends and families gathering for a joyful celebration sweetened the event. Everyone loves a wedding, especially the Greeks. It seemed as if the whole town showed up in one way or another to offer help or congratulations.

The wedding ceremony took place on a terrace perched above the cove. The stunning Greek bride, with her long dark locks of hair draping over her flowing white dress, rivaled the beauty of the setting. Alyssa is the oldest of Nick and Marina's three daughters, all of whom are beauties, for which Nick jokingly takes all the credit.

The weather was typical for Crete in August. A hot Greek sun burned in the cloudless sky and the sea shimmered at its touch.

The canopied terrace gave some shelter from the sweltering heat of the day, but the occasional touch of a passing ocean breeze brought the sweetest relief of all.

After the short ceremony, the guests walked down the stone stairs to a waterfront taverna and settled in for a long, sumptuous dinner. Gauzy white curtains swayed in the breeze, and bright pinks and reds of bougainvillea blossoms decorated the tables. It looked like a picture postcard of *The Best of Greece*. A bounteous spread of succulent Greek food covered the white tablecloths. Robust red and crisp white wines from the acclaimed Manousakis Winery in Hania flowed freely. As the sun set, the heat of the day melted into cool dusk on the water.

But what stood out as the crowning moment for many of us were the tributes made at the reception. This was not the typical chain of cheesy toasts and raunchy roasts offered by tipsy siblings or college roommates looking to outdo one another with feeble attempts at humor. Rather, this was a class act of thoughtful and articulate sentiments, shared with the intention of honoring the recipient and peppered with just enough humor to lighten the mood. The speech of the day award went to Nick, the father of the bride. His eloquent speech honoring his daughter and new husband included a beautiful tribute to his wife. He had everyone choked up, including himself.

The traditional wedding feast ended around 11:00 p.m., and then the partying began in earnest. A Greek wedding is the party of all parties, an all-night affair of eating, drinking, dancing, and carousing until the sun comes up. The mixture of nationalities represented by the groom's and bride's families made the party a melting pot of Western and Greek music. The groom (a non-Greek) impressed us with his performance of a traditional Greek dance called the *sirto*. As the night deepened, the energy heightened, and we linked arms with other guests to join in Greek circle dances. We fumbled through the complicated footwork, but no one seemed to notice, probably because everything looks better after a few drinks. Besides, the mood was one of exuberance and fun at all costs. At 3:00 a.m., Richard and I retired, exhausted, to our hotel room, leaving the rest of the crowd to finish off the party that was still going strong.

The next morning we awoke to a shining example of a Greek summer day. The coolness of the morning was quickly dissipating into summer's heat. The cloudless sky promised a sweltering August day. Aromas and sounds from the tavernas below us wafted up to our balcony. After a breakfast of fresh squeezed orange juice and *spanikopita*, we decided to jump in the water for a morning swim.

Two fisherman were cleaning the morning's catch on a their boat docked at the pier. As we approached the end of the pier, we saw a sea turtle hanging around pilfering scraps of fish tossed overboard by the fishermen. I slipped into the water and quietly approached the turtle. She ignored me for the most part, and seemed more interested in the morsels of fish thrown to her from above. She glided around and under the boat, swimming and diving, with me close behind. She even accepted a little stroke on her mossy back as we were paddling around together. Eventually she headed out to open waters beyond the large cove.

Nick uses a word when he is describing something that has elements of wonder and surprise: *magical*. Magical indeed. A wedding weekend of shared laughs and precious memories with friends in the stunning setting of Loutro.

And dancing with a sea turtle was the icing on the cake.

SIMPLICITY

The people of Crete harbor no pretences. Their food and homes are simple and unadorned and their emotions are raw and honest. The Cretan culture unapologetically exudes a timeless authenticity.

As an American looking in from the outside, I see how my culture is one of stressed excess. In contrast, the culture on Crete is one of shared simplicity. Like many people in this world, the common Greeks don't have a lot, but they still manage to share what they have with a smile. Over the past twenty-five years, the Greek economy has gone from bad to worse, as any household will attest. The men talk about it in the local kafenios over a cup of muddy Greek coffee or a shot of strong raki; families join together on a rooftop patio and complain about their financial misfortune in the same breath as laughing over a funny memory.

Suffering is shared as readily as a plate of biscuits and a coffee. Neighbors help each other and families stick together.

They tell stories, laugh, love, and fight in small spaces and at loud volumes, but they do it in community.

My next-door neighbor was a poor farmer who always left fresh vegetables on my stone wall. Seven watermelons, two bushels of *gigantes* (big butter beans), and five giant cauliflower heads appeared at intervals, making me wonder how many people he thought I was feeding. No matter. It was his generosity that counted.

In spite of the very serious economic woes in Greece, many moments of goodness and humor occurred in a given day. In our village of Horafakia, I met a tough old gal named Niki with a heart of gold. She was one of the few women in the village who knew how to drive a car. The fact that she didn't own a car didn't stop her from offering rides to neighbors and friends. It wasn't unusual to see her behind the wheel of her ancient tractor generously schlepping local women to the market and back. The sight of her wobbling down the road with a trailer full of village women was sure to bring a smile to the hardest of faces.

As I drove out of our village on the Akrotiri one summer day, another sight took me by surprise. I rounded a corner and came up behind a rather portly older gentleman walking on the side of the road. He was outfitted in a non-descript pair of gray shorts, old slip-on sandals, and he was shirtless. Nothing unusual, except the fact that he was covered from head to ankles in a thick layer of white fuzzy body hair. A thought flashed through my mind as I passed him that he was certainly an impressive example of the quintessential older Greek man, but nothing prepared me for the sight in my rear view mirror that nearly caused me to run off the road. Besides his barrel chest and great belly that was carpeted in the same mass of hair as his back, he was sporting on his face, the biggest, whitest, fuzziest handlebar mustache I've ever seen. And as he strutted on his bowed legs confidently down the road, I could almost hear him thinking, *Zorba ain't got nuthin' on me!*

The simplicity of scenes like these made living on this crazy island not only tolerable but magical. And the slower pace made more room for observation and contemplation. I was more aware of what God means when He says, *"Be still, and know that I am God" (Psalm 46:10).* I learned the vital art of slowing down. Sometimes it drove this frantic American crazy, but most of the time I loved it. It didn't take long for Richard and me to settle into a pleasant evening routine during the warmer months. Most evenings, as he cooled down after his bicycling commute from the base, we sat on the shaded front terrace and shared a small *mezethes* (appetizer). Our favorite was a slab of feta cheese swimming in a pool of green olive oil sprinkled with sea salt and oregano and washed down with a glass of refreshing white wine. Eventually, we moved to the back terrace as the sun lost some of its heat and relished in dinner and the view of the sun setting over the water. We lingered over succulent fresh food, talked about the day, and watched the stars come out. I rarely got much done in the evenings, but I was actually a better person for it.

We've learned that we can live very comfortably with a fraction of our belongings, that life doesn't revolve around our e-devices and overcommitted agendas, that there's always time for a long walk and or a long lunch (even if it's Greek style—three hours,) and that a smile and an easy "hello" is the universally understood sign of kindness, no matter where in the world you are. Maybe it's the water. It just seems second nature to slow down, ease in, and immerse yourself in the moment.

Years later, I was still trying to wrap my brain around life on Crete. As we settled into the groove of daily work and play, I started relaxing and enjoying just living the moments that made up interesting days, weeks, and years on this curious island.

Richard once asked me, "What is it about this place that you love so much?"

I had to think about that one. "My favorite thing about Crete is the simplicity of life. There's something about it that resonates in a deep place within me."

Today, I forgot my wallet when I went to my local market. Giannis (the grocer) shrugged when I got to the checkout and told me to just come back later with the money. I reflected on other ways this relaxed way of life presented itself:

- *My doctor doesn't have a receptionist, or a computer, or a long list of drugs for me to sample. He examines me thoroughly, writes notes on a small pad of paper, and recommends a holistic remedy available from the local pharmacist next door.*

- *My surprise birthday party is thrown together in a week. No elaborate decorations, no fancy drinks; just a bunch of friends enjoying fantastic food and fellowship.*

- *Greek fast food = souvlaki on a stick with yogurt dip and homecut fries.*

- *Best of all - A typical day's wardrobe is simply a sundress, a pair of sandals, and no makeup.*

I'm sitting at my favorite secluded spot at the Agia Triada monastery. My back is against the age-yellowed plaster wall and my eyes are drawn upward towards the bell tower on the church. All is silent, and I feel the worries and concerns of the day evaporating into the warm Mediterranean air.

> *"Be still, and still moving"*
> —T. S. Eliot

BIG FAT GREEK FOOD MAGIC

Toula Portokalos: Ian is a vegetarian. He doesn't eat meat.
Aunt Voula: He don't eat no meat?
Toula Portokalos: No, he doesn't eat meat.
Aunt Voula: WHAT DO YOU MEAN HE DON'T EAT NO MEAT?
[*the room goes silent*]
Aunt Voula: Oh that's ok, That's ok. I make lamb!
(Scene from *My Big Fat Greek Wedding, 2002*)

Lingering over a tasty meal with friends and family, savoring the delicious moments of good food and good companionship, is Greece at its best. No wonder the Greeks take their time at the table. They have long practiced the secret to good health and longevity through the Mediterranean diet. But there's more to a meal than just well-prepared food that yields healthy results. Taking time to honor the important things in life is the seasoning that makes all the difference. Relationships are a priority. For the Greeks, it's clear that a good meal shared between family and friends is the formula for health and happiness on a daily basis. In the Cretan household, meals are not merely a nutritional necessity; They are an expression of love.

Ask anyone who has been to Greece, and Crete in particular, and they will likely tell you that after sampling Mediterranean cuisine, they are hooked. And the delectable flavors that pass over the palate are second only to the nutritional benefits for the body. Thus, the Mediterranean diet has earned the distinction of being the best diet in the world. The simple nutrition and preparation of a Mediterranean meal flies in the face of hoity-toity designer, fusion, or haute cuisine. There is only one rule of thumb: fresh and simple. The Cretan land produces an abundance of gastronomical delights: olive oil, honey, herbs, wild greens, traditional cheeses, and nuts are only a few, all locally grown, of course. There is nothing like a home cooked meal on a Greek island. When you ask a recent vacationer what the best thing was about his or her trip to Greece, they will inevitably say, the food. But that flavorful *moussaka* or savory lamb *stifado* doesn't just start in the kitchen. It starts early in the morning at the *laiki* (farmer's market.)

The laiki is the center of activity most Saturday mornings as locals and tourists alike stroll from booth to booth sampling and selecting all varieties of fresh gastronomical delights. Seasonal fruit, vegetables, and homegrown herbs straight from the farmer provide a palate of colors and scents. The cheeses on display include vats of feta and *mizithra* (a tasty soft cheese reminiscent of ricotta) and wheels of *graviera* (a hard sheep cheese that boasts sweet and fruity flavors.) Bottles of unlabeled local red wine (which is really brown wine of questionable taste) teeter on one side of a wobbly table. Other bottles of that clear, potent moonshine called *tsikoudia* or *raki* hold down the other side of the table. Raki is described both as a delightful digestive or a gut burning jet fuel depending on the distiller. Sandwiched in between the displays of colorful produce are tables adorned with local thyme honey, fresh flowers, and simple glass bottles of homegrown, cold pressed, bright green, extra virgin, pride of the Cretans: olive oil.

The laiki is a sensual pleasure of sights, sounds and smells. Saturday is the big market day in the center of Hania although there are laikis every day of the week tucked away in different locations around the city neighborhoods. My personal favorite was the Thursday morning laiki in the neighborhood of Nea Chora on the west side of the old harbor in Hania. It was smaller, less crowded and in a beautiful setting under the tamarisk trees that shaded the seaside street. It's everything you would expect from a European farmers market, but more frenetic and chaotic. A cacophony of noises rises up from the vendors shouting out their daily specials amidst the constant hubbub of different languages spoken by Greeks, tourists, and expats.

On a typical Thursday morning, most of the shoppers were older women dressed in their traditional black garb carrying numerous heavy bags of potatoes, oranges, and various vegetables. It was a common sight to see them trudging up the street with bags of produce hanging off their strong arms. They looked like they were going to feed an army. I quickly learned that most of the women did in fact cook a huge meal every Sunday for an army of family and friends that gathered around the food-laden tables on their outdoor patios.

It didn't take me long to purchase a wheeled trolley for packing in all my treasures. I always seemed to buy too much, but we never had trouble consuming the fresh produce and cheese I hauled home. Big, red tomatoes for €0.70 per kilo (that's 2 1/2 lbs!) and a huge hunk of feta fished out from a 50-gallon vat were always on my list. After a morning of shopping for freshness, I was rewarded with bags and bags of seasonal veggies and fruits at a next-to-nothing cost to me. I could hardly wait to get home and get started on some kitchen creations.

Crete may have its share of problems, but it never lacks for good, fresh, abundant food. You have to look pretty hard to find bad food in any taverna or market place. The mountain villages especially have some phenomenal traditional Cretan cooking straight out of mama's (or baba's) kitchen. No menu is necessary. You are invited to step into the kitchen where they will lift the lids on all the pots and pans filled with Greek delights for you to sample and choose.

Back in my own kitchen, as I empty my bags from the laiki, the fragrance of "fresh" wafts up from the array of color on my countertop. Lemons smell like the color yellow, and tomatoes have that heady fragrance of freshness, even before you slice into them. I LOVE to chop, mince and dice. There is something relaxing and satisfying about carefully chopping ripe red tomatoes or a bunch of fragrant cilantro. Richard and I make good cooking partners. I chop, he stirs and tastes, and tastes. . . and tastes some more. He also does a bang-up job of cleaning up after me. Our favorite dinner is a medley of fresh veggies marinated in olive oil and balsamico and roasted on the grill.

I know this sounds crazy, but I love it when I find a snail in my bunch of spinach. That's how I know it's organic and fresh. When I bring home my load of produce from the laiki, sometimes I find little hitchhikers, which end up being freed into my yard rather than cooked up in a pot. That's one of the reasons I don't have a recipe for snails. That, and the fact that I just have never developed a taste for them.

I gained a whole new appreciation for simple, slow cooking, using fresh, seasonal ingredients. And I learned that good cooking is so much more than what you put in a pot. It begins with careful choices of ingredients, unhurried preparation, and lots of practice. Nothing good comes out of being in a hurry. So much of the essence of a meal (or a moment) is lost to multitasking madness.

So it is with relationships. Just like cooking, good relationships don't just happen. A superb chef starts with the best ingredients, nurtures the process over time, and is brave enough to make mistakes. In the testing kitchen of life, there will be many successes and many failures. But always there will be the aroma of the sweet and the savory. My best friend from Crete, Marina, and I still share a special bond between two women who love the Lord, love our family, and love to cook. Good friendships seasoned with laughter, peppered with love, and slow cooked with patience yield the sweetest memories.

OPA!

A GREEK WEDDING

"I'm so happy you are still here!" Katerina announced.

Richard was having no luck finding a job back in the States, so for the time being we were "stuck" on an island in the middle of the sea, two years longer than we expected. I must admit, our third year was the hardest. We felt as if we had one foot in Crete and the other in Colorado with no promise of returning home in the near future. But somewhere in the middle of our fourth year, we turned a corner. Crete started feeling like home—a place we belonged and a place we shared with friends like Katerina. She and her family embraced us like their own, hosting us for dinners, grape stomping, orange picking, and other Greek festivities. Our years on Crete were enriched largely because of this big-hearted family.

Katerina sidled up to me and repeated, "I'm SO glad you're still here!" I could tell something was up. When we first moved to Crete, Katerina was a single Greek woman married to her engineering job on the navy base. Slowly, a long childhood friendship blossomed into new love. She was dismissive as first and rarely talked about the new relationship, but today she was glowing.

"Sifis and I will be married this summer," she said with a big smile, "So, you see, now you *have* to stay for our wedding."

"Oh, Katerina, that's wonderful! I'm so happy for you!"

And so, on a sultry July evening in Hania, our Greek "daughter" Katerina married her childhood friend, Sifis. Unlike the wedding in Loutro, this was a strict Orthodox wedding with all the traditions and trimmings. But just like the wedding in Loutro, it was a magical night of celebration full of the emotion and promise of new beginnings. When an American thinks about a Greek wedding, images from the film *My Big Fat Greek Wedding* usually come to mind. But the Greek orthodox wedding is an ancient sacred ceremony filled with deep symbolism and serious reverence for the holy act of marriage.

The Orthodox sacrament of marriage is unique in many ways. The ceremony has remained almost entirely unchanged since its origination centuries ago. One interesting note is that the bride and groom do not exchange vows. Instead, their presence before God, the priest, and the congregation signifies their wish to be joined in marriage and to accept Christ into their new home.

Family and guests gathered outside the same church where Katerina's parents were married decades before. Sifis stood with his parents and sister awaiting the arrival of his bride and holding her bouquet of flowers. A car drove up to the steps of the church and Katerina emerged, escorted by both her parents. They made their way up the path where the groom awaited near the altar. The look of adoration on Sifis' face was almost as mesmerizing as the radiant bride. They seemed unfazed by the sweltering heat that was melting the rest of us.

Sifis and Katerina made their way through the courtyard towards the altar as their families and friends settled into chairs or stood under the shade of the trees. I turned to Efigenia, a Greek friend of mine, and asked her to explain what was about to transpire.

"The ceremony begins with the betrothal service, or ring ceremony," she whispered. The priest led the bride and groom to the altar where the *koumparos* (best man) and the *koumpara* (maid of honor) joined them. He then blessed the rings and Katerina's koumpara placed them on the right ring fingers of the bride and groom after passing them back and forth three times between their hands.

"That symbolizes that they were forever entwined," she continued. "Most of the rituals in the ceremony repeat three times to represent the Holy Trinity." I watched, mesmerized as the priest said a prayer to seal the rings, and placed his vestment over their crossed hands.

"Now, we move into the marriage ceremony. The candle standing next to the altar represents Jesus, the Light of the world," she explained as the couple lit their candles from the center flame. "He will guide them and bless their new life together." The priest chanted three prayers and joined their hands together.

"This next part is my favorite," she said with a smile. "It's called the crowning. Those flowered circles are called *stephana,* or wedding crowns."

"What do they symbolize?" I asked.

"The crowns represent the glory and honor bestowed on them by God, and the ribbon that links the crowns together represents the joining of two souls into one household, like their own kingdom."

The priest placed the *stephana* first of Sifis' head and made the sign of the cross as he spoke a blessing three times over him.

Efigenia translated for me.,"The servant of God, Sifis, is crowned unto the handmaiden of God, Katerina, in the name of the Father, and of the Son, and of the Holy Spirit. Amen."

Beautiful, I thought. I was near tears when he moved to Katerina, placing the crown on her head and repeating the same blessing over her three times. Sifis' koumparos then exchanged the crowns between the couple three times as the priest read two Scriptures: a passage from the epistle to Ephesians which states the commitment and responsibilities of marriage partners, and the Gospel reading from John which includes Jesus' first miracle at the wedding in Cana.

Efigenia's whisper startled me out of my reverie, "Now is the time for the drinking of the sacrament, the common cup." When it was time for the couple to sip the red wine from the sacrament cup offered by the priest, a moment of light humor transpired at the altar. The height discrepancy between tall Sifis and the much shorter priest resulted in an awkward tipping of the cup and the wine nearly missed its mark. A few relaxed chuckles broke the otherwise serious mood.

At the end of the ceremony Sifis and Katerina took their first steps as a married couple in the traditional Dance of Isaiah. As the priest chanted a series of hymns, he led the couple, still joined together by the ribbons of the stephana, around the altar three times. The circle represents the eternity of marriage. He held the Bible out in front symbolizing that they will follow the Word of God in their lives together.

The solemnity of the previous rituals changed to smiles and lightheartedness as the guests threw rice and wished them a long and happy marriage. The priest removed the stephana from their heads and used the Bible to uncouple their joined hands representing that only God is able to divide this marriage. He finished with a blessing and a prayer to seal the marriage.

The crowd erupted into applause and Efigenia smiled at me exclaiming, "Now the real celebration begins! Are you joining us at the reception?" I assured her we wouldn't miss it for anything, and we moved towards the well-wishers that gathered around Katerina and Sifis. A nearby table was adorned with wedding favors or tokens of gratitude from the bride and groom to their guests. Each guest received a small toile-wrapped bag containing an uneven number (symbolizing that the couple cannot be divided) of *koufeta* (sugar-coated almonds) and miniature bottles of *mastic liqueur* from the groom's home island of Chios.

After the solemnity of the marriage ceremony, everyone was ready to cut loose and celebrate. The typical Greek wedding reception is a study in extravagance, and this one was no different. Over 250 guests enjoyed endless food and drink while taking a break only to join in festive Greek dances like the *Kaslamantiano*. "Opa! Opa!" Jubilant exclamations from the dancers floated on the breeze above the music. The cool night air in the outdoor garden was a welcome guest and the party continued until dawn.

As we left the reception in the early hours of the morning, I looked back at Katerina and Sifis and silently wished not just happiness but something more permanent. Joy. In Greek, *Chara* (pronounced Ha-RA), meaning a deep feeling of inner gladness, delight or rejoicing; a profound peace not dependent upon circumstances.

DIVING DEEP
A LESSON IN JOY

*"Joy does not simply happen to us. We have to choose joy
and keep choosing it every day"*
—Henri J. M. Nouwen

I laid on my towel on the cool sand after my usual morning swim. The total distance across the cove and back was roughly one mile, but the view through my goggles was so captivating that it never seemed that long. I timed my swim so I finished just as the morning sun crested over the cliffs of Stavros that loomed above the east side of the cove. This morning was quiet and still.

As the sun rose over the ridge, its heat moved slowly over my body and melted away the goose bumps on my salty skin. Stavros was my favorite beach. It was well within biking distance of our home and seldom crowded. Located on the northern-most tip of the Akrotiri peninsula, it encompasses Blue Beach to the west and Stavros Cove to the east. I spent many moments that stretched into hours in and around the waters of Stavros.

My skin prickled as I sat up, almost dry now thanks to the ever-increasing heat of the sun. I reached into my small red cooler and pulled out my breakfast: Greek yogurt drizzled with local thyme honey, seasonal fruit, almonds, and a bottle of fresh-squeezed orange juice. Sitting on the beach under my striped umbrella, I spent some time in the pages of a favorite book, looking up once in a while to observe the other early morning swimmers, mostly older Greeks, bobbing up and down in the water close to shore. Their routine was always the same. They entered the sea slowly but deliberately, splashing the cool water on their arms. Then gently lowering themselves, they treaded water for at least 30 minutes while carrying on long conversations with their friends. It was like watching a geriatric water social. I never saw a Greek, young or old, who had a decent swimming form, but they could sure tread water longer than anyone I know.

After some reading and ample daydreaming, I made my exit around 10:00 a.m., when the morning solitude was interrupted by noisy sunbathers. I headed for home, making a detour through town to the other side of Stavros to beachcomb the big sandy beach that stretched out on the north shore of Crete. I walked at the water's edge past a thatched-roofed taverna called *Iliovasilema* (the Sunset.) Most locals just knew it as Malika's, named after the curly-haired French woman who owned and operated it. Her simple beach hut was an inviting oasis in the sands of Stavros. Giant spool tables under palm-thatched umbrellas provided a welcome respite from the sun. Many days, after a quiet evening swim in the sea, Richard and I loved to sit with our toes in the sand, feasting on the remarkable sunset view over the water and sipping on a cold beer.

The Sunset was quiet this early morning, but Malika was up preparing for the day's customers. She smiled and waved as I walked towards her.

"Hi, Malika. What's on the menu today?" I asked.

"Oh, the usual. I have a nice *papousakia* (stuffed eggplant) that is very good. And of course, the shrimp risotto."

Malika's creations from the tiny beach kitchen included samplings of French, Greek, and Moroccan flavors. The menu consisted of daily items scribbled on a small blackboard and presented to hungry patrons by Malika herself, or friends helping out. My personal favorites were the *roka* (arugula) salad, grilled *aubergine* (eggplant) and risotto. Richard's plate always included her special mussels cooked in wine.

"How do you come up with your menu?" I asked, sitting on a deck chair. "It's not your typical Greek fare."

I was curious about how she ended up starting a business on a Greek island beach when she was clearly not of Cretan origin.

She didn't seem to be in any hurry, so she sat down next to me and began sharing her story in her musical French dialect.

"I was born and raised in Burgundy, France, but when I was young, I used to come to Crete for my holidays. I loved the sea and the calm way of life. Something I can't explain drew me back here time after time."

I nodded in agreement. Beneath its surface warts and imperfections, an energy of pure equilibrium flows in the veins of Crete.

"How did you end up immigrating here?"

She smiled wryly, "For the love of a man. Many women who holiday on Crete fall in love here. It is very common. When I was 21, I met a young Greek man, he swept me off my feet, and now here I am. After we married, I knew I couldn't live in the city, and I love how peaceful it is here in Stavros. When we moved to this village, I got the idea to open the beach taverna. It was very hard to get through the red tape of Greek bureaucracy, and many locals didn't want a foreigner opening a business here. But that was over 15 years ago and I'm still here. Now I do what I love—cook, swim, and raise my daughters in this peaceful place. It *is* beautiful, no?"

We were silent as we gazed over the sand to the calm sea of early morning. When I looked back at Malika, I saw *meraki*, that Greek word that describes the essence of your soul that you put into your work. Love, creativity . . . joy.

On many summer evenings, Richard rode his bike from work and met me at Stavros Cove. In my car were his swim trunks, a couple of cold beers, and a picnic. During the hot summer months, the trunk of my car was affectionately known as Mel's Toy Box. It was completely outfitted with everything we needed for a summer outing. In May, I stocked it with a supply of beach towels, extra swimsuits, an umbrella, beach blankets, games, sandals, sarong, sunscreen, and hats. Our little Honda was a mobile sandbox all summer. In October, at my husband's insistence, I reluctantly cleaned it out and vacuumed up enough sand to build my own beach.

The most important "toy" in my box was my snorkel gear. I never went anywhere near the sea without it. In the late afternoon and evenings of summer, the only escape from the intense heat was in the cool clear water. Snorkeling was a great way to pass the time while staying cool.

And it's also a good way to lose track of time. The sights and sounds of land dwellers disappear. Just below the surface of the water dwells a different world of mesmerizing tranquility. Its hypnotic flow of ever-changing light and motion can make time stop. Snorkeling was like church for me. It was my place to be alone with God and feel his presence around me like a warm liquid blanket. My position of prayer was floating on my back in the buoyant sea and gazing upwards towards the cloudless sky.

Sometimes I had to go deeper to find what I was looking for. It was tempting (and easier) to tread water on the surface and observe the distorted depths from above. Snorkeling is like that. But things can be cloudy and imperceptible from the surface. Only in diving deep can they become clear and defined.

I spent many hours diving in Stavros Cove and other places to collect sea urchin shells of all sizes and colors. I surprised a small shy octopus and a fierce-looking fanged moray eel, both lightning-fast in their escape. I saw more of what the sea had to offer when I was diving *in* it instead of just floating *on* it. There is a world of difference between being an observer to being a participant.

Many times in the sea and in our lives, out of either comfort or fear, we avoid diving deeper. We opt to remain on the shore viewing clear skies, calm seas, and playful children on the beach. Predictable and safe. That is until the storms move in.

Years ago, a storm of huge proportions rocked my life. In 1992, another island on the other side of the world suffered a massive typhoon. Houses, roads and complete mountainsides in Taiwan were swept away in its fury. A van loaded with local businessmen and one American was traveling down a winding and remote road in the aftermath of the storm. That one lone American was my father.

Heavy rains caused the road to collapse into a sinkhole filled with rushing water. In the dark of the night, the driver didn't even see what was ahead of him. The van and its occupants plunged into the depths of that cavernous hole. Six men, including my father, lost their lives.

The phone call no one ever wants to get came that afternoon at my mother's home. I had dropped by for a quick visit and was waiting to say goodbye while she answered the phone. When her face went pale, I knew something terrible had happened. The days and weeks to follow were consumed with consolations and preparations, both of which I welcomed as distractions from my own grief. But grief is not something you avoid by skirting around it. The only way to get through grief is to go right through it; dive right into the middle of it, feel it, embrace it, and be tender with it.

It wasn't until after Dad's memorial service weeks later that I felt like I was drowning in grief. A stormy sea of emotions choked me every time I tried to breathe. It was in this whirlwind of anguish that God reached down and saved me from myself. But he had to take me deeper to do it.

On one particularly fragile morning, I was deep in sorrow and feeling frustrated that I couldn't pull myself together. I wrote about it in my journal:

As I cried out to God, a sudden peace washed over me as a word picture played over and over in my mind. In this scenario, I could see myself attempting to stay afloat in a sea racked by wind and waves. The sky was dark and the water was tumultuous. Every time I tried to stay on top of the water, the raging waves thrashed and beat me down. But as soon as I let go and allowed myself to sink deeper I found respite and peace from the chaos above me.

Somewhere deep down I understood that God was trying to tell me something. The storm on the sea represented my emotions. God created every emotion in me the same as he created the storm and the sea and it was all good. But if I continued to fight and "live" in my emotions I would get nowhere and only end up exhausted. I needed to dive deeper into the peace of God; the "peace that passes understanding" outside of circumstances and the emotions they stir up. At that moment, I trusted and quit struggling. The deeper I dove, the more peaceful the water became. Finally, I was safely resting on a solid rock at the bottom of the sea. Somehow I could breathe and as my "dream" ended, I was not afraid anymore.

> *"On Christ the solid rock I stand,*
> *All other ground is sinking sand,*
> *All other ground is sinking sand."*
> — (Hymn by Edward Mote 1834)

Bottled up in the waters of Crete are favorite memories of snorkeling and discovering new and marvelous life at the bottom of the sea. Many times we see life from the surface. We observe those things that are blatantly obvious to the naked eye and claim our short-sightedness as vision. But there is a bigger picture. God lifts the veil of distortion and bids us to dive into a deeper reality to discover the depths of his love.

The sea reminds me of his nature: Unfathomable depths and indescribable beauty. Sustenance for life. A mystery of mysteries. A safe place to wrestle with questions and discover peace - a peace that passes understanding. And joy . . . joy amidst the waves of doubt that pound on the shores of change.

fULL HARVEST

"*Don't judge each day by the harvest you reap,*
but by the seeds you plant."

— Robert Louis Stevenson

LIFE INTERRUPTED

HELPLESS BUT NOT HOPELESS

*"We walk by faith and not by sight because there are
places to go that cannot be seen and the scope of our vision is
too small for our strides. Faith is not a denial of facts – it is a
broadening of focus. It does not deny the hardness of guitar strings,
it pluck them into a sweetness of sound."*

— Rich Mullins

F our women, a Brit, a Greek, and two Americans, sat at table
in the café Koukouvaia perched high on a hillside overlooking
the old harbor of Hania. A warm spring breeze shifted the gauzy
curtains that hung from the corner of the terrace. Evening settled
over the city as the reflection of harbor lights began to fill the
silent sea below. This was a perfect ladies night out. Dear friends,
good wine, stellar view—I was suddenly overwhelmed with a
feeling of lighthearted peace. *All is well*, I thought to myself.

That was about to change.

Later, I returned home still basking in the feeling of happiness
that comes from spending time with people you love. I opened

the door to the house and sensed something was wrong as soon as I saw my husband's face.

"Call your daughter. Right away."

"What's happened?" I asked with my heart in my throat.

"Just call her. Kai has been in an accident."

Trembling, I dialed her number in Colorado and she answered after the first ring.

"Mama, Kai's been hurt . . . really bad. We're all at Children's Hospital and he's in surgery. It's really bad." Her voice broke and in between sobs she described the seriousness of her nephew's injuries. I listened, trying to ignore the knot in my stomach that was quickly becoming nausea.

Earlier that day, the 90 pound family dog suddenly attacked our baby grandson, nine-month-old Kai, pinning him to the sofa and crushing his skull in his powerful jaws. Even in her panic, his mother was able to lock the dog in the bathroom, wrap a towel around Kai's head and dial 911. The Flight for Life helicopter whisked him off to the ER in Denver and twenty-four medical personnel worked frantically to save his life.

Trying desperately to stay calm and hide the panic in my voice, I encouraged her to be strong and pray.

"We have a crowd of friends and family already here around us doing exactly that," she said. "I have to go. The doctors are coming. I'll call you right back." And she hung up.

Only then did the emotions come over me like a flood. My legs gave way and I fell into Richard's arms sobbing uncontrollably. I've never in my life felt so helpless, so far away from the people I love.

As the minutes and hours ticked by, I was glued to the sofa with my computer open to Skype and the phone next to me, desperate to receive any more news of Kai and his anxious parents, my son and his wife. The time zone difference of nine hours was insignificant, as I stayed awake all night waiting for news during those first critical hours when he teetered between life and death. In between the brief conversations with family and friends, I spent a sleepless night in that otherworldly place of deep prayer, hovering despair, and a puzzling but distinct sense of peace. Each time the phone rang I jumped and grabbed it, longing to hear a familiar voice that would magically decrease the distance between me and my family, only to hang up again feeling farther away than ever.

Over the hours, my initial feelings of shock and denial gave way to the overpowering sense of urgency that I needed to get back to Colorado immediately. I would have hiked across land and ocean if I could have. In the early hours of my morning (late night in Colorado), the phone rang again and I heard my daughter's tired voice, "He's out of surgery now. The doctors worked on him for six hours to control the bleeding and . . ." her voice broke, ". . . pick pieces of his skull out of his brain."

My stomach lurched as she composed herself and continued.

"His heart stopped twice. It was too dangerous to keep working on him, so they bandaged up his head and he's in the ICU now."

A glimmer of good news, I thought to myself. *He's still alive!*

But then the bad news.

"They didn't give us much hope. It's one of the worst traumatic brain injuries they've seen. He isn't expected to live through the night."

We cried and held onto each other through the phone with words of love and comfort—a poor substitution for being together. The whole tragic circumstance seemed to increase the miles between us.

The next few days while Kai held on to a thread of life, I put everything and everyone in motion to secure my flight from Crete to Denver. I will forever be grateful for my friend Marion taking over this overwhelming task for me, and three days later I boarded a flight headed for the States via Athens, London, New York, and finally Denver—over 20 hours with layovers. I hadn't slept since the accident and I was bone tired. I hoped to find some much-needed rest on the long journey, but found it impossible to sleep. As soon as I drifted off, a little voice would worm into my head, reminding me indelicately that I should prepare for the worst.

Twenty hours was a long time and anything could happen. I might be going to a funeral in Denver instead of the hospital.
What if he does live? What will his life look like?

To silence that anxious voice, I prayed. I screamed in my head to God. I wrestled with doubt, fear, worry, anger, and exhaustion. Finally, I let go and waited for the peace he promises. I wasn't disappointed. Almost immediately, a Scripture jumped into my mind and wouldn't go away, "We walk by faith, not by sight."

I felt like God was telling me, "You will see, hear, sense scary things when you see Kai. But don't give in to fear. I am doing a great thing. The doctors are doing their best, but ultimately, I am the Healer. I am holding Kai in my arms, close to my heart."

"He gathers the lambs in his arms and carries them close to His heart" (Isaiah 40:11).

It was then I realized that he was truly in control and wanted to remind me, *"Do not fear, for I am with you; do not be dismayed for I am your God. I will strengthen you and help you; I will uphold you with my righteous right hand"* (Isaiah 41:10). Not looking behind and not looking too far ahead, I knew he would give our family what we needed: grace for the moment. For the first time in four days, I closed my eyes and fell into a deep sleep.

Children's Hospital, Denver Colorado
Sitting in a bedside recliner in the Pediatric Intensive Care Unit is not the place anyone wants to be. No one could ever design a chair that would even come close to providing the comfort one needs. Sweet baby Kai lies with his life in the balance. The sorrow in this room is so thick I can hardly breathe.

Kai's mama and papa were constantly at his bedside, talking to him, stroking him, loving him, while dealing with a full gamut of emotions - fear, sorrow, anxiety, guilt mixed with moments of light and hope. During the following hours and days at Kai's bedside, I had ample time to reflect on life in general, and specifically, how my experience living in Crete prepared me for this moment. I realized that many truths were born in me and grew to maturity during the five years we lived abroad. Truths that changed me forever, like deepened patience, tolerance, compassion, quietness, a sense of a bigger picture, and a profound conviction that this world is not my true home. It's because of that firm "knowing" I can be content wherever I live. But more than anything, I knew that God planted a new faith within me that rooted itself in my very core: faith in myself, in others and in him. I was like a tree being blown around with the wind, broken in places but still strong. That faith was now being tested and so I put one shaky foot in front of the other and walked into the unknown.

Over the next few weeks in the ICU, Kai endured a series of brain and plastic surgeries, and miraculously, he continued to improve. I lived at the hospital and became quite accustomed to hearing Kai described by medical personnel as "the miracle baby." Some days it was two steps forward, another step back, and I can't remember how many times we heard the words, "He's doing better, but he's not out of the woods yet." He was not alone on this journey though. Someone was always keeping vigil at his bedside. If love alone could heal him, he would pull through with flying colors. Each morning we thanked God that he made it through the night, and each night we prayed for sweet healing sleep. And when he awoke the next morning, we celebrated. That was the routine. Surrounded by family, friends, and the caring staff at Children's Hospital, he improved to the point where, after a month he was released from the ICU.

The big day came and he was transferred to the rehab floor where the hard work would begin. All of his ICU nurses shed tears of joy along with us as they kissed him and wished us well. A long train of little red wagons filled with everything from suitcases to dozens of stuffed animals made its way from the ICU to the sixth floor. As the nurses settled Kai into his new room, I whispered a prayer of gratitude that he was here—alive. He still had SO far to go but he was a strong little boy with a Miracle Maker on his side.

This day was also the day for my return flight to Crete. Kai was in good hands, and I knew that his parents would need me more when he was finally released from the hospital to go home. So, with a heavy heart and a hundred prayers, I said tearful goodbyes to Kai and my family.

When Richard met me at the airport in Hania, we held onto each other for a long time. I felt whatever strength I had left drain out from me in the comfort of his big arms, and I wept in that safe place. It was a bittersweet reunion, relieved to be with my husband but sad to be away from Kai. A huge sigh escaped my lips on the drive home. Richard looked over at me and we both knew. It was time to go home to Colorado.

With a renewed sense of urgency, we put into motion all the big and small tasks of moving from our Crete home to our Colorado home. Two years prior, we were more than ready to return home, having had our fill of Cretan chaos, but in the ensuing months and years something had changed. We came to treasure our time on Crete and surprisingly began to think of it as home. So, it was with considerable sadness that we packed up and said our goodbyes.

A NEW SEASON
CRETE'S LEGACY

"The seasons remind me that I play one small part in a bigger picture—that there is a pulse, a sequence, a journey set into motion by the very hand of God Himself."

— Karen Scalf Linamen

When I look at photos of Kai and the rest of family and friends in Colorado, I know it's time to return to the States. I am truly excited to see what God has planned for us there. But right now, as I look over the calm blue morning sea of Crete and take in the sounds of cicadas' songs and the lilt of Greek conversation around me, I feel a tug at my heart that feels strangely like homesickness when I think of leaving this place.

If someone were to ask me what is the best advice I could give to make the most of life on a Greek island I would have to answer, "Expect the unexpected." This vigilance of heart yields great rewards. First, you are more apt never to be surprised and therefore save yourself and others from weird emotional outbursts. Secondly, you find yourself challenged to reframe your thinking, which I've heard is good exercise for the brain. Lastly, it's never boring, seldom predictable, and always an adventure of sorts. It all depends on how you look at it. Of course, I've found that my positive outlook significantly increases if I've had a good night's sleep and a strong cup of coffee, followed by a brisk swim in the sea. I can always think better after that combination.

But sometimes the unthinkable happens and in a single instant our lives are changed. Those pivotal moments burst into our reality, crushing our neat little world and leave us gasping for breath. Time is suddenly measured in relation to when the fateful event occurred. Life as it was known before, ceases to exist, and a new unwelcome reality moves in. Suddenly we face the challenge of fleshing out the truth that life isn't what happens to you, it's what you DO with what happens to you.

On our last day on the island, I wrote in my journal:

As I look back on the five years we've lived here, I realize that this comfortable feeling I have is because I'm settled in here and have allowed this place to get under my skin. This feels like a home away from home. Sure, I'll never be Greek; I'm an American; but somehow I've managed to ease into the interesting lifestyle of Crete, which is characterized by a slow, easy pace punctuated by bouts of extreme chaos. Hania, Crete, will always hold a special place in my heart mostly because of the people that have richly colored my experience here.

What did I learn in my short five years in Crete? From the simple and curious to the profound and serious:

1. Hospitality is more about opening your heart and home than throwing a great party.
2. Making time to visit a friend or extend kindness to a stranger is time well spent.
3. Eat REAL food. If it's wrapped in plastic or preserved in cardboard, avoid it.
4. Organized chaos works as long as everyone know and abides by the rules (i.e., driving habits).
5. Be prepared to laugh a lot at yourself if you're brave enough to try to converse in Greek.
6. America is a great country, but not the greatest. No country can lay claim to that. We can all learn from each other, but that would take a great deal of humility.
7. The only true Christian nation is not identified within borders, but rather by the diverse community of rag-tag believers around the world who simply desire to be followers of Christ.
8. I'm stronger than I thought I was, but I realize the more I learn, the less I know.
9. Sometimes reluctant beauty rests in the hard places.
10. Digging deep produces rare gems:
    power in simplicity,
      freedom in the unencumbered,
        joy in living for each moment,
          and peace in a slower pace.

I realize that in opening my heart to a new culture, I have also opened myself to the vulnerability of heartache. I have let Crete and the people here get under my skin, and it all has become a part of me, shaping and changing me in ways I never imagined. So, it's not without an ache of loss that I think about leaving this place. God has blessed us immeasurably in our experience here, especially with good friends. But I know that he has prepared us, fashioned us, tested us, and refined us in this place of extreme harshness and beauty for his purpose.

EPILOGUE

*Unless you expect the unexpected, you will not find it, for it is
hidden and thickly tangled.*

— Heraclitus of Ephesus, *Greek philosopher*

"What did you learn from living on Crete?" That's the question I'm asked the most. Followed by, "What is your favorite memory?"

My response is usually, "Do you have a few hours?"

So many memories revolving around people, places, and adventures fill my thoughts. Nearly every weekend on the island found us on some road or bike trip seeking out new experiences. And when we weren't traveling, we were spending precious moments laughing, crying, eating, and storytelling with so many of our dear friends.

But perhaps the best memories are those wrapped up in the simple brown paper of everyday life. Memories captured in the playful joy of children on the beach, long evening walks with the dog, card games and sweet *freddo* cappuccinos at Koukouvia Café, fresh Greek salads at the seaside, girls' days and nights out, outdoor cinema gatherings at our house on warm evenings, moonrise over the water, a long silent swim in the sea, sweet scents of jasmine and gardenia, and long dinners on the terrace with friends. Even the little surprises like two tiny, sick stray kittens wandering into our yard were laced with sweetness. These memories and more were my comfort and companions as we moved back to Colorado after almost exactly five years on Crete.

> *Moving to Europe was one of the most difficult things I've done, but not as difficult as moving back to the States. Packing up all our belongings and navigating through all the details was nothing compared to packing up all my memories and navigating through all my emotions. I remember the feeling of bewilderment when someone said, "You must be so excited about going home!"*

> *Where is home? If "home is where the heart is" then my heart must be in pieces. A little here, a few there, left behind like an intimate goodbye letter propped up on the mantle. It's hard to come home when you've been home somewhere else. But in time, the leaving gives way to the coming and a measure of peace settles in. That's when you know you're home —again. Until the next time and it repeats all over.*

When we first returned to the States, most of my island yearnings were replaced by concern and care for Kai and family. After the accident, the doctors warned us that Kai had essentially reverted to the skills of a newborn. He was starting over. He learned how to breathe on his own, drink, eat, move all his limbs, sit up, vocalize, and best of all, smile and laugh like the old Kai. He celebrated his first birthday in the hospital with cake, ice cream and a slew of party guests. He continued to improve with amazing strides that left even the most seasoned doctors scratching their heads, and by August, he returned home. We arrived back in Colorado two weeks later. It was the sweetest homecoming we could have imagined.

Richard and I were both still confident in our decision to move back because, as we liked to say, "Family trumps everything." But as we settled in to our familiar life in the States, I began to feel strangely out of place—like I was still searching for my real home.

I couldn't quite put my finger on why I was feeling so conflicted—comfortable and yet deflated—when I returned to the States. and then it occurred to me: The familiarity of American life makes it predictable . . . "normal" . . . almost boring. Living on Crete meant life at a snail's pace, out of season food not available, inconsistent business hours, weekly business closures because of yet another strike or holiday celebration, no regard whatsoever for rules in regards to traffic or queuing up. But these aggravations were rooted into the very reasons it was such a great place to live.

Much of my disjointed feeling after returning to the States was due to navigating through some serious reverse culture shock. Everything was bigger and faster and I began to realize that the small-town European culture just fits my personality better. But the close proximity of our precious family was priceless, and so I treasured every moment with them. The challenge was how to blend the best of Crete with the best of America. I had to be intentional to preserve and practice the pieces of Cretan life I had come to love—the slower pace, a stronger sense of God's presence amidst the busyness of daily life, an afternoon nap or cup of tea, a better diet—and gently mix them into American life.

> *Sometimes the homesickness for Crete settles in so deep that I can taste the yearning and want to run there. Sometimes I feel like I don't belong here. But truthfully, I don't belong there either. Sometimes I think if I'd never left here I wouldn't have to deal with such a mucky mess of emotions. But, if I had never stretched my faith and moved into the unknown, I would not be the person I am today – changed forever. And I realize that a few of us lucky ones can say we have many homes – each one has left its imprint on our hearts and influence in our lives. And the pangs of homesickness are a reminder that God has emptied us into the lives of others and vise versa.*
>
> *Bottom line, what we have discovered is that you can't live your life to the fullest if you are paralyzed by the past or fearful of the future. All any of us have is this present space in time and we are charged with filling it with wisdom, compassion and gratitude. What a pity to miss the beauty of the here and now because we are blinded by the "if-only's" or afraid of the "what if's."*

So with that in mind we forge ahead with great expectations of the next adventure, deep gratitude for the dear friendships left behind and a fresh wonder of the beauty in each moment.

Happy trails, kalo taxidi (bon voyage), and God bless.

Melanie and Richard

APPENDIX I

MY FAVORITE GREEK RECIPES

Authentic Greek Salad (NO lettuce please!)

3 firm, ripe tomatoes, chopped
2 cucumbers, sliced
1/2 green pepper, sliced
1/2 red onion, quartered and sliced
1/2 cup kalamata olives
1/4 cup olive oil
Big slice of feta
Vinegar, salt, and pepper to taste
Pinch of oregano

Mix all in a bowl and top with feta slice, plenty of olive oil, and a dash of vinegar. Sprinkle with oregano.

Baked Feta

8 oz. chunk feta
1 small tomato
1/2 onion
Green, red, and yellow peppers
Kalamata olives
1/4 tsp. red pepper flakes
1/4 tsp. oregano
1/3 cup olive oil
Salt and pepper

Lightly coat ovenproof dish like a small crock with olive oil. Place feta in crock. Top with minced vegetables, red pepper flakes and oregano. Season lightly with salt and pepper. Drizzle with remaining olive oil.

Bake in 350 oven for 30 minutes or until bubbly. Serve with crusty bread or crackers.

Graviera with Herbs

8 oz. graviera cheese (substitute Jarlsberg or Gruyere)
1 medium tomato
1/2 cup extra virgin olive oil
1/2 tsp. thyme
1/2 tsp. oregano
1/2 tsp. rosemary
1/2 tsp. freshly ground pepper
2 tbs. parsley
1/2 tsp. sea salt
1/3 cup chopped walnuts

Cut the graviera cheese into strips or cubes. In a large bowl, finely chop the tomatoes and add the salt, half of the olive oil, the thyme, oregano, and rosemary. Mix and add the cheese. Mix again and add the rest of the olive oil, parsley, and walnuts.

(For a sweet variation–top graviera cheese with honey and crushed walnuts.)

Tzatziki *(Yogurt/cucumber dip)*

2 cups whole-fat Greek yogurt
1 large cucumber
3 large cloves garlic, minced
1 tsp. anise (or 1 shot ouzo liqueur)
1 1/2 tbs. olive oil
Salt and pepper

Finely grate peeled cucumber onto clean dishtowel. Squeeze out excess water (I like to save it for a refreshing addition to lemonade or ice water.) Mix cucumber and remaining ingredients into yogurt. Chill for 1 hour. Serve with fresh baguette bread slices or pita wedges.

Dakos *(Greek crostinis)*

12 barley rusks (or crispy crostini bread slices)

2 ripe tomatoes, grated (cut tomato in half; hold skin side, and using coarse grater, grate pulp only; discard skin)

1 cup mizithra cheese (or soft feta)

Extra virgin olive oil

Oregano

Ground pepper

Sea salt

Arrange bread on platter and lightly brush tops with olive oil. Top each with a dollop of grated tomato and cheese. Sprinkle with a pinch of oregano, pepper, and salt. Drizzle with olive oil.

Lemonato Kotopolo *(Lemon Chicken)*

3 cloves garlic

1 whole chicken, cut up

2 potatoes per person

1 tsp. fresh ground pepper

1 tsp. mustard

1 tbs. oregano

2 tsp. salt

Juice of 2 lemons (plus zest)

1/2 cup olive oil

1/2 cup water

Peel potatoes and cut lengthwise in fourths. Place in large cooking pan. Lay chicken pieces on top. Cut one garlic clove in half; slice a small hole in each breast and insert 1/2 garlic clove. Cut others in half and lay around pan. Add oregano and pepper.

Dissolve mustard in lemon juice and zest and pour over chicken.

Add salt, oil, and water. Cover with foil and bake at 350 degrees for 1 hour.

Uncover, return to oven and bake 10 minutes, or until golden brown.

Chicken Soup with Avgolemono (Egg-lemon) Sauce

Soup:
3 lb. roasting chicken or chicken pieces (bone in is healthier!)
2 to 2 1/2 quarts water
1 carrot chopped
1 onion chopped
1 stalk celery chopped
1 cup cooked rice or orzo
Salt and pepper

Sauce:
2 eggs
3 tbs. fresh lemon juice

Wash chicken and place in heavy pot in water to cover. Add pepper, carrot, onion, and celery. Bring to a boil, cover and simmer over low heat for 2 hours, or until chicken is tender, adding salt to taste during last hour of cooking. Remove chicken and keep warm. Add rice or orzo and simmer until done. Take meat off bones and place back into the pot.

Make the Avgolemono sauce:

Beat eggs well and gradually beat in lemon juice. Add two cups hot, strained broth *slowly* to egg sauce, beating constantly. Return to soup to heat and stir until thickened.

Although I never took an organized cooking class while we lived in Crete, I had many opportunities to shadow a few culinary experts in their kitchen. I learned from the best.

The women who cooked up their delicious creations in our favorite lunchtime taverna, Kouzina, were always willing to share their recipes and tips with me.

Chickpea Salad *(from Kouzina Taverna)*

2 cans garbanzo beans (chickpeas)
1/2 cup onion, chopped
1 stalk celery, chopped
1/2 cup chopped cilantro or parsley
1/2 cup extra virgin olive oil
6 tbs. lemon juice
Salt and pepper to taste

Combine and chill or serve at room temp.

Maria at the Sunset Taverna in Horafakia cooked up THE BEST mushroom pie on the island. She willingly schooled me in the details of her recipe, but I never could get it right. I'm convinced that the slices of mushroom pie I consumed in her taverna overlooking the sea had some kind of magic ingredient she kept secret.

Maria's Mushroom Pie *(from Sunset Taverna – Horafakia)*

4 cups mushrooms, thinly chopped

1 onion, grated

¼ cup olive oil

2/3 cup whole milk

2 ½ cup grated mozzarella cheese

1 egg, beaten

1 packet puff pastry

Wash and rinse the mushrooms very well and squeeze to remove excess water. Chop into small pieces. Sauté the onion in the oil and add the mushrooms, leave to cool.

Add the milk, cheese, eggs and mix. Place the filling in an ovenproof dish (approx 35 cm x 20 ; 14 in x 13 in) . Lay a sheet of puff pastry on top and brush with olive oil. Score into portions and bake in an oven at 375 degrees for about 30 min., until the pastry is golden brown.

My Greek friend, Eri, spent an entire afternoon in my kitchen preparing a winter soup with meatballs. It all started out in the morning as we perused through the laiki in search of the freshest ingredients available. When we returned home later that morning, our arms laden with plastic bags full of veggies, she got right to work. As she flitted around my kitchen chopping, sautéing, and tasting, I knew I'd better write my observations down if they were going to end up in my recipe box. But when I tried to pin down measured amounts, she shrugged and said, "A little of this, not too much of that."

I did manage to at least jot down the ingredients before she scooped them into the big pot on the stove. This soup is guaranteed to chase away the winter chills.

Cretan Winter Soup

Meatballs:
1 lb. lean ground beef
1 onion, chopped
1/2 cup cilantro or parsley, chopped
1 egg
1 tsp. cumin
1 tsp. oregano
1/2 cup uncooked rice
1/2 jalapeno, minced
1 small potato, peeled and grated

Mix well with your hands and form into 2-inch balls.

Soup:

2 large peppers (red and green), chopped

3 green onions, chopped

1 shallot, chopped

3–4 small zucchini, cut in thirds

3–4 small potatoes, peeled and cut in large pieces

3–4 carrots, cut into large chunks

1/2 cup olive oil

2 tsp. dill weed

1 tsp. coriander seed

1 1/2 C long grain rice

In large soup pot, sauté peppers, onion and shallot in olive oil. Make meatballs and place on top of cooking veggies. Add remaining vegetables and slowly add 4 cups water or vegetable broth to pot. Bring to boil. Add rice; boil 20 minutes; Stir gently. Add dill and coriander. Reduce heat to simmer. Make avgolemono sauce (egg-lemon sauce).

Avgolemono Sauce:

Whisk juice of 1 lemon slowly into beaten egg. Add hot broth from soup a little at a time while continually whisking until there is about 1 cup. Pour sauce over top of soup. Don't stir. Jiggle pot gently to mix.

I learned quickly that the best cooks never use a recipe; at least in Greece. They have time-tested recipes passed down through many generations, and culinary magic seems to be in their DNA. My friend, Marina was originally from South Africa but immigrated to Crete after marrying Nick, her Greek love. She claims that she never knew how to cook, and Nick is quick to share funny stories of surviving the first few years of marriage around their table. But her determination and natural ability, mixed in with some of Nick's own culinary expertise, produced some amazing results years later. Any time we were invited to share a meal at Nick and Marina's home, we always said yes. One of my favorites from their kitchen was a slow cooked beef stew.

Beef Stifado

2 lbs well-marbled beef cut into small portions
1/2 cup of olive oil
1 large onion chopped
1 clove garlic chopped
1 carrot chopped
2 grated tomatoes (or 1 can diced tomatoes, undrained)
2 tbs. tomato paste
1 cup of red wine
Salt, pepper
1 cinnamon stick
2 cloves
2 bay leaves

Braise meat in olive oil. Remove from saucepan.

Add onions and garlic to saucepan and sauté.

Return meat to the pan and add in wine and remaining ingredients. Simmer very slowly for about 2 hours. Check if meat is soft. Serve with potatoes and a salad.

And no Cretan cookbook would be complete without a recipe for Boureki, a classically Cretan casserole you won't find anywhere else in Greece, much less the world.

Boureki

4 zucchini squash, sliced thinly
4 white potatoes, sliced thinly
1/2 cup fresh mint, chopped
1 tsp. oregano
Salt and Pepper
2 cup flour
4 cup mizithra cheese (substitute 3 cups ricotta and 1 cup crumbled feta or goat cheese)
3 eggs, beaten
3 cup milk
1/2 cup olive oil
sesame seeds

Combine flour, salt, oregano, pepper, and mint and toss zucchini and potatoes to coat. In separate bowl, combine cheese with beaten eggs and mix well. Arrange a layer of 1/3 zucchini and potatoes with 1/3 of the cheese mixture. Continue to layer until all veggies and cheese have been used. Pour milk and remaining olive oil over the boureki. Top with sesame seeds. Bake at 375 for 1 hour, or until top is golden brown and veggies are tender.

APPENDIX 2

THE INSIDE SCOOP FOR THE SAVVY VISITOR
TRUTH, TRIVIA, AND THE PURSUIT
OF HAPPINESS IN CRETE

Crete is the place where ancient mythology collides with deep-rooted history, and the result is a heady mix of legend, religion and tradition. This multi-faceted island has the power to leave indelible mark on your heart and soul. And vice versa. Information is power, so educate yourself before you visit Crete to ensure you and those you meet along the way will have good memories of your visit. A few notes to tuck inside your mental suitcase:

Taverna: (Not to be confused with an English pub or tavern):
A Greek restaurant or café.

Kafenion (café): (Not to be confused with a *taverna*):
Greek men's hangout for morning coffee and gossip as well as a friendly game of backgammon (Tavli). In earlier times, there

were always at least two kafenions in each village no matter how small. The exterior paint of the kafenion indicated the political leanings of the owner so you could choose your own preference and therefore try to avoid political arguments. Modern day kafenions allow women but most women prefer to get the gossip from the men when they return home. Plus, they are busy cooking up the next meal for their huge family.

Greek worry beads:

That constant chatter and clinking you hear in many cafes and Greek gatherings are the music of the komboloi, the Greek version of "worry beads." Usually the komboloi is a constant companion of the older male generation, but a few younger men have also mastered the art of intricate flips, tricks, clicks.

Unfinished houses:

If you're wondering *what's with all those rebar rods sticking out of the roofs,* you will get a variety of answers, including the tax-evasion theory. But more accurately, here's the answer: Greeks build only what they need for the present and leave the rest unfinished to add on to at a later date. Most Greeks provide independent living quarters for their daughters but not for their sons, who are expected to marry a girl who gets a house from her parents. It's not unusual to see a family house with rebar sticking out of the roof waiting for the next floor to be added as their daughter approaches marriage. Imagine if you have more than three daughters – looking to build a high-rise apartment?

282   UNIQUELY CRETE

Greek restaurant service:

Greeks consider it rude to impose on their patrons until summoned over. So what you may consider bad service is, in fact, their respect for your privacy. They will take your order and give suggestions, but only if asked. After delivering the food, they will leave you in peace to leisurely enjoy your meal and companions. They are never in a hurry, and they don't expect their patrons to be either. Complimentary dessert and raki come before the check.

Tips are not necessary because they are usually included in the price but 10 percent is reasonable if you are impressed with your experience. If you over-tip, you may find yourself sitting at the bar at the insistence of your waiter as he treats you to more drinks than the tip covers.

Theft:

The Greeks are horrified at the idea of stealing, thus theft is very, very rare in Greece. Unfortunately, petty theft is a problem in tourist areas but not at the hands of Greeks. Usually poor gypsies or immigrants are the culprits. A Greek person would be too humiliated to steal another person's belongings. However, it is not below them to cheat a little. In fact, it is considered business savvy to inflate prices. Sometimes referred to as "tourist tax."

Cash society (especially in restaurants):

It would be very unusual to see Greeks splitting the check; one person usually insists and always pays cash. If a Greek person invites you to a meal or drinks, it is not customary to offer to pay your portion. Conversely, if you invite them, you are expected to pick up the tab.

Most shopping is paid for in cash with the exception being in the tourist areas. Almost always you will expect to pay cash in a grocery store. Paying bills is always a challenge because the queues can get quite long in the utility offices.

Family:

Family helps family at all times, under all circumstances. Financial crises have burdened most of the Greek population, but they always take care of their own. Even the smallest and most modest of homes will take in a destitute relative for an indefinite period of time—and no one ever goes hungry as long as there's a mama or yia-yia in the kitchen. Homelessness is not the norm in Greece, and for those unfortunate souls who have no family, the Orthodox church has a wide network of food kitchens to serve them.

Invitation to a Greek home:

If you are privileged enough to be invited to a Greek home, bring flowers or sweets. Wine is not the usual gift as the Greeks are very proud of their own supply. Greeks are very generous people. If you are invited into their home, be careful to avoid overcomplimenting any of their household possessions. You may end up taking them home with you.

Name Days:

Greek Orthodox children are usually named after a saint whose name was passed down through the family, specifically their grandparents. For example, our friend Katerina (Ekaterini or Catherine) was named after her mother and that name has since been passed down to her own daughter. Her name day is November 25th. Name days are celebrated more often than birthdays. A visit to the person's house to offer best wishes is in order. The host family provides a table of delicious treats to enjoy together. You should bring a gift that will be opened later by the name day celebrant.

Surnames and first names:

Greek women always keep their surname and don't take their husbands unless they wish, and then it would be hyphenated.

Many first names have an "s" at the end that is dropped when addressing someone or speaking directly to him/her (i.e. Yiannis – Yianni; Nikos - Niko.)

Proper spellings:

Is it Chania, Hania, Khania or Xania? Answer: All of the above. There are multiple spellings for the same city or location. Remember that Greek is one of the two oldest languages (along with Chinese) to survive the modern world, so chalk it up to another Lost in Translation moment and don't overthink it.

GMT = Greek Maybe Time:

Time is of no particular significance to the Greeks especially on an island. This applies to bus schedules, doctors' appointments, hair appointments, shop hours . . . you get the idea. The Greek people don't live by the clock. This practice is foreign to the Western world and Type-A Americans, but delightfully refreshing. As a rule of thumb, the following applies:

Morning = sunrise till noon

Afternoon = no earlier than 6 p.m.

Evening = no earlier than 9:00 p.m. (which is when the typical Greek dinner begins)

Siesta = Sacred relaxation time is loosely between 3:00 and 6:00. Everything shuts down (except in tourist areas)

Beach time:

Expect to pay for sun beds (usually two loungers and an umbrella go for €5–€8 for the day.) Some tourists think this is a ploy to get money from them. On the contrary, it is a legitimate business. Someone has paid a sum of money to the municipality and "purchased" that section of the beach for a season. He is responsible to provide chairs and umbrellas and keep a clean beach area. Pick out your spot and he will approach you momentarily to collect your fee. Fees vary depending on location of the beach and facilities available (bathrooms, tavernas, showers, etc.)

And speaking of picking your spot, Greeks don't understand the concept of "personal space," so don't be surprised if, after laying your towel down on an empty section of sand away from the crowds, you return from your swim to find a large Greek family camped out within inches of you. When I asked a friend why this was so prevalent, she responded a little tongue in cheek, "Since you got there before them, they assume you found the best spot."

Favorite Beaches:

Hands down my favorite Crete beach is Gialskari for so many reasons starting with the location near my favorite beach town of Paleohora. See Chapter *Beating the Heat in Crete*

My favorites closer to home on the Akrotiri near Hania include:

Stavros Cove - gentle waters, nice big beach, tavernas, killer cliff views, family friendly

Blue Beach - secluded small beach with accommodations and a great taverna – Thanasis.

Kalathas – a local favorite. Shallow waters on an expansive beach. Eat at the beachside taverna, known simply as Tula's after the woman who cooks up a fantastic Greek lunch, then swim out to the little island off shore.

Marathi - Another local family favorite includes a marina, two beaches, and the best seafood taverna around.

Other beaches around the island that offer everything from seclusion to a hopping nightlife include:

North coast: *Platanias, Agia Marina, Kolymbari, Kalyvas, Almyrida*

South coast: *Loutro, Preveli, Glyka Nera* (Sweet Water), *Damnoni, Sougia*

West coast: *Balos, Falassarna, Elafonissi*

Proper greetings:

Kalimera (Good day): Morning through 4:00-ish

Kalispera (Good afternoon): 4:00-ish – 9-ish

Kalinikta (Good night): After 9-ish and usually as a farewell

Parakalo: Please (also You're welcome)

Efharisto: Thank you

Yia-sas: All purpose greeting and farewell all day

Yia-sou: Same as above but to one person familiar

Stokalo: Familiar farewell to close friend or family literally meaning, "Go well."

And of course the most endearing words in any language:

Se agapó . . . I love you

CPSIA information can be obtained
at www.ICGtesting.com
Printed in the USA
LVHW111137100219
606878LV00008B/10/P

9 781949 021172